MIDWEST Scoops

Finding the region's best ice cream parlors and custard stands

FANCY
PANTS
PRESS

Series Editor
Michael McGarry

Brand Identity and Book Design
Alusiv, Inc. | Philadelphia, PA | www.alusiv.com
Richard Cress, Mark Wills, Rebecca Phipps

Illustrations
Sandy Knight

Cover Photography
Beverly Poppe

Contributor
Megan O. Steintrager

Production Consultant
Jim Bindas, Book Productions LLC

Copy Editor
Sharon Parker

Editorial Assistant
Maia Homstad

We would like to thank Ryan and Eric Berley of the Franklin Fountain in Philadelphia, PA, John and Stephanie Reitano of Capogiro Gelato Artisans in Philadelphia, PA, Hossein Rahimian of McConnell's Ice Cream in Santa Barbara, CA, Barb Zapzalka of The Pumphouse Creamery in Minneapolis, MN, and Ben Scholtz of Mallard Ice Cream in Bellingham, WA, for generously providing access to their shops and ice cream for our photographic purposes.

Printed in China.

Library of Congress Control Number: 2005920014
ISBN-13: 978-0-9749118-1-6
ISBN-10: 0-9749118-1-X

Bulk purchases are available at special discounts. For more information please visit our website.

FANCY PANTS PRESS

Published by
Fancy Pants Press
P.O. Box 8902
Minneapolis, MN 55408
info@happybellyguides.com
www.happybellyguides.com

10 9 8 7 6 5 4 3 2 1

Happy Belly Guides are an essential resource for people seeking an alternative in today's franchise-laden dining landscape. We believe that memorable gastronomic experiences are found at locally or regionally owned establishments, where tasty food takes precedence over profit. While finding these authentic eateries in one's hometown is difficult, discovering them in an unfamiliar setting is nearly impossible. For that reason, each of our guides is extensively researched, carefully written, and stylishly designed with the primary goal of leading readers to beloved yet overlooked locales: the best independent shops, shacks, restaurants, cafés, and parlors of the culinary world.

Happy Belly Guides help you find the food you rightfully crave, served by the people who make it best. So go ahead, pick up one of our guides and put a smile on your tummy.

HOW TO USE THIS GUIDE

The purpose of this guide is to help readers find and eat the best ice cream, gelato, custard, and other frozen delicacies in the Midwest. Each section highlights a group of states, arranged geographically, moving west to east. Shops within large metropolitan areas are grouped together even though some may fall outside of official city boundaries. At the end you'll find a glossary of selected ice cream terms. Additionally, throughout the guide you will find special sections under the heading EXTRA SCOOPS. These sections provide the background on the history and myths surrounding this long-revered treat as well as interesting information regarding all things ice cream.

We realize that navigating through unfamiliar cities is confusing, so for that reason we have included directions to each address. We have painstakingly attempted to include accurate operating hours, but please keep in mind that hours frequently fluctuate from week to week and shops may close for months at a time without any notice. Phone numbers are listed, so please feel free to call in advance.

Many shops have information online and we encourage you to look them up using the listed web addresses. If you are hungering to taste a reviewed shop's flavors before your next road trip, we have marked the places that offer online ordering with this minipint symbol: .

Finally, although we stand by all of the selected entries, we realize that a few good shops may have escaped our attention. If you frequent a great shop that you think merits mention in future editions or want to comment on any of the entries, please feel free to send us an e-mail at **info@happybellyguides.com** or post a review at **www.happybellyguides.com.**

ACKNOWLEDGEMENTS

My belly and I would like to thank everyone who helped me on this book and series:

All the ice cream parlor owners, managers, and scoopers who have given me their time and who continue to work their best to please our palates;

The Happy Belly all-star advisory team;

Jeanne Sloane, Andy Steiner, John Manning, Ann Prichard, Dimity McDowell, Sheila Ortona, Professor Kulny, Mark "Czech Mate" Krajan, Nicolle Nelson, John Larson, and Joey "Jelly Roll" Bartolomeo, scribes and specialists who help spread the word of the Happy Belly;

Jeannie and Graham Parlin, Johnny Trimble, Harry and Mary Manning, Karl Omdahl, and Charlie Mullin for their help in tracking down the Midwest's best;

Jim Ellison, Shannon Jackson Arnold, and Malcolm Stogo — ice cream gurus all;

La Regina, my best customer, and Papa, for his farmer's wisdom;

Catherine, her stylish connections, and her new husband Oliver "Cover Shot" Prichard;

Godmother Sarah, "Minivan" Mike, princess Bridget, and the mighty Austino;

Clan Kordonowy, for providing my nonice cream rations;

Ice cream models and tasters: Anna, Astrid, Iris, John, Lydia, Isabelle, Sabine, and Henry;

All the friends and family who bought the gelato guide even though they had no plans to visit Italy — and especially those who made plans to visit as a result of reading it;

James, my chunky baby boy and future ice cream aficionado;

and of course Ray, my very own three-scoop sundae, loaded with all the toppings.

Menu

STATE SECTIONS

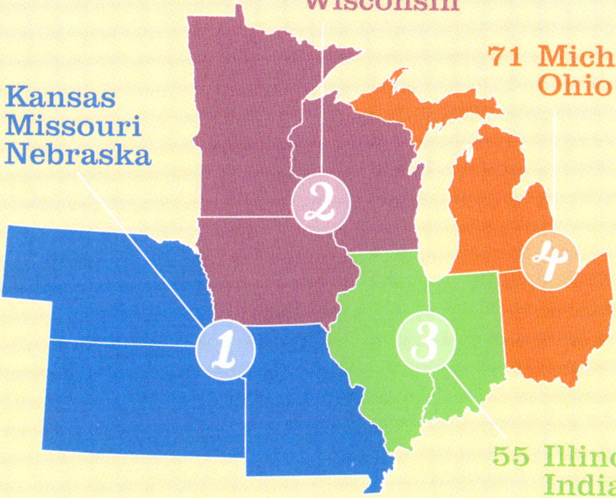

OTHER SECTIONS

UNITED WE SCOOP

Ice cream is the ultimate American treat. George Washington considered it his favorite food, Thomas Jefferson had his own recipe for vanilla, and Ronald Reagan commemorated it by proclaiming July National Ice Cream Month. A good deal of our affection for ice cream stems from the simple fact that it is delicious and refreshing, but the ice cream phenomenon is more than just a gastronomic infatuation. Our love of ice cream is also rooted in an appreciation of the people who dish out this delight and the ice cream parlor settings that continue to bring communities together.

Not so long ago customers had personal ties with several of their local merchants, visiting neighborhood fruit stands, butchers, bakeries, and other stores on their daily shopping rounds. Over time most of these specialty shops have been phased out by supermarkets or relegated to once-a-week farmers' markets. Ice cream parlors were able to survive this conglomeration, however, and continue to foster relationships with the communities they serve. Granted, one can buy ice cream at a grocery store or visit one of the omnipresent national ice cream chains at a nearby strip mall, but all American cities of scale have at least one hometown or regional ice cream parlor. These shops create environments where individuals can mingle in a way that is rare in today's society. They are one of the few places where loitering is encouraged, kids are welcome to run and play, and adults may actually strike up a conversation with a stranger.

These revitalizing atmospheres are the direct result of the work of a special breed of people who choose to make ice cream their calling and fulfill their own American dream. Whether started by newly arrived immigrants over a century ago, or recently founded by people looking to change their careers and lives by launching their own small businesses, each shop reflects the ambitions of its owners. Whatever these ambitions may be, from building the next ice cream empire to simply offering tasty flavors and contributing to their community, the men and women behind these shops are a talented bunch. To be successful, all must combine business acumen, good people skills, and a mastery of the art of making delicious ice cream. Their stories are as unique as their shops, and they provide a backdrop for this guide.

Additional backdrop is provided by the towns and regions throughout the Midwest that play host to the ice cream parlors and custard stands reviewed here. Each city and state is different and these independently owned shops reflect these distinctions. What seems perfectly normal in Chicago, like their penchant for serving ice cream alongside Italian beef sandwiches, would seem ludicrous in Milwaukee, where **custard is king and giant butter-burgers** are the preferred red meat option. St. Paul has a shop that offers an extra tiny scoop for people too **"Minnesota nice"** to ask for a free taste, and a parlor in small-town Wilton, Iowa,

serves only one item in the morning, peanut butter toast, before switching to homemade ice cream in the afternoon. These unique shops all have a common Midwestern atmosphere, however, with a region-wide love of dairy and a not-fit-for-either-coast kindness uniting them together. Additionally, they each have fervent devotees, each of whom *knows* his or her favorite is the best. We think they are all right.

In order to find the exemplars of the ice cream parlor tradition, the Happy Belly staff looked through books, newspapers, magazines, websites, directories, and other sources for any mention of good ice cream. We called local information bureaus and ice cream retailer associations. Mainly, however, we relied on the advice of a network of friends, strangers, and shop owners, each eagerly making at least one suggestion. Once we had a refined list, I jumped in my car and visited all the shops my belly could handle, trying when possible to visit the flagship shop because these are typically the most authentic. I spoke with customers, interviewed owners, and ate more pints than Ben and Jerry combined. This research uncovered the best of these shops, and those are the sites that are reviewed in the following pages. Each holds a prized position within their communities, is run by dedicated owners and staff, and serves unforgettable ice cream. So please, visit as many of these shops as you can, taste the best ice cream in the land, and...

find your happy belly...

ICE CREAM BASICS

As its name suggests, ice cream is a frozen food made from a mixture of dairy products. Federal law mandates that ice creams contain at least 10 percent butterfat, before the addition of nonessential ingredients, and weigh a minimum of 4.5 pounds to the gallon. These are only base levels, and it is in the deviation from these minimum standards that varying ice creams achieve different echelons of taste.

KEY ELEMENTS

Butterfat Content The amount of butterfat in the base of a particular ice cream determines the richness of a flavor — the higher the butterfat content, the richer the taste. The best ice creams usually have a butterfat content between 12 and 18 percent, but there are worthwhile ice cream variations, such as gelato, that contain a lower percentage.

Overrun Percentage Overrun is the percentage increase in volume of ice cream due to the incorporation of air beaten and blown into batches during mixing and freezing processes, greater than the amount of mix used to produce that ice cream. A significant amount of overrun is necessary in ice cream, because without air the dairy-based mixtures would be rock hard and unservable. Too much overrun, however, leads to a fast-dripping, unfulfilling scoop. The best ice creams have an overrun level of about 50 percent or less (meaning that 25 percent of the product is air), whereas mass-produced brands, seeking to maximize profit margins, run as high as 100 percent.

Additional Ingredients Like any other food product, ice cream can only be as good as the ingredients that are used in its production. Every shop has different standards, but the best are willing to charge a little more for each scoop in order to make sure that what's inside is worthy of your palate.

QUALITY

Depending on their methods and recipes, shops, farms, and dairy plants create ice cream that falls into the following quality categories:

Super-premium With a high butterfat content (typically 16 percent or higher), low overrun percentage (around 30 percent), and use of the highest quality ingredients. Most of the parlors in this guide serve ice cream that falls into this segment.

Premium A step down from super-premium in all aspects, but still worthwhile.

Regular/Economy Ice cream that just meets the minimum levels of butterfat content and overrun percentage and typically uses medium-grade ingredients. A fine purchase if you are looking to buy in bulk at a supermarket, but not acceptable from your neighborhood parlor.

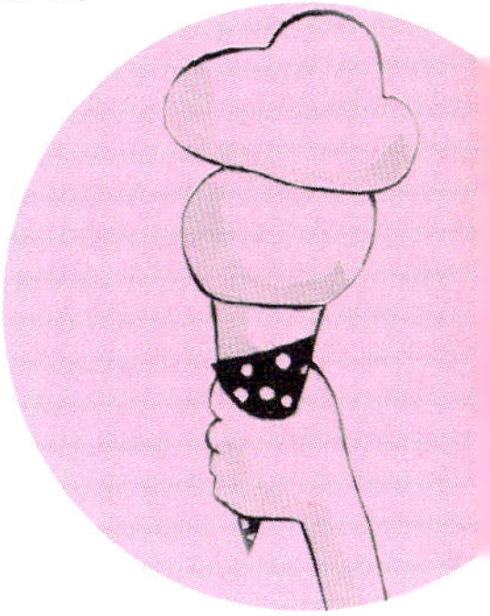

Section 1

KANSAS MISSOURI NEBRASKA

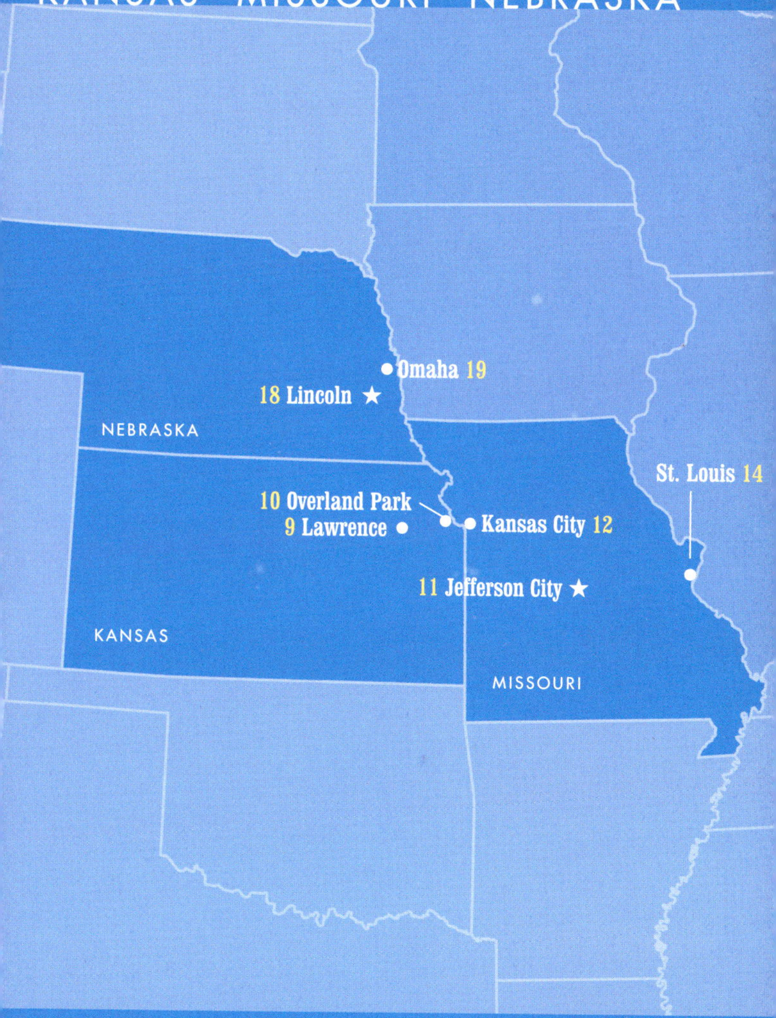

LAWRENCE

Sylas and Maddy's

ADDRESS 1014 Massachusetts St.
PHONE/WEB 785-832-8323
HOURS Sun–Thu 12p–9:30p, Fri, Sat 12p–10:30p
DIRECTIONS *Two locations. The Massachusetts St. shop is in the center of the town's main drag between 10th St. and 11th St. The other shop is in Olathe, a suburb of Kansas City.*

Nestled between restaurants, shops, and cafés, SYLAS AND MADDY'S is the place to go for ice cream when in Jayhawk country. The shop, whose two owners chose the name in honor of two pets, a tabby and a terrier, pays attention to every detail, from the bright walls featuring hand-painted cones and sundaes to the tiny desks perfect for kids gorging on two-scoop fantasies. The shop's homemade waffle cones are delicious, especially the ones lined with chocolate, sprinkles, and/or nuts, and the placement of malt balls at the bottom as a means to prevent dripping is much appreciated. Into these cones is placed sublime ice cream which I heard praised from as far away as Iowa City. SYLAS AND MADDY'S motto, "add a new flavor to your life," is meant to encourage customers to try their unique creations and participate in the fun by submitting flavor suggestions — the best of which are selected to be flavors of the month and named in honor of their creators. The shop's signature items are **da bomb**, containing cookie dough, oreos, and chocolate flakes, and **gold dust**, a mixture of Snickers, Oreos, and caramel, but for me nothing beats their pure **peaches 'n' cream**.

CHALLENGE:

Created as an homage to Lawrence's favorite chant, the ***rock chocolate Jayhawk*** *flavor, a vanilla base with bits of brownies, fudge pieces, and fudge swirl, has become the shops best seller. Rock chocolate Jayhawk, go KU!*

OVERLAND PARK

Custard's Last Stand

ADDRESS 10138 W. 119th St.
PHONE/WEB 913-338-5737 / www.custardslaststand.com
HOURS Sun 12p–10p, Mon–Thu 11a–10p, Fri, Sat 11a–12a
DIRECTIONS *Four locations and two franchise shops throughout the greater Kansas City area. Overland Park location is in the Highland Plaza shopping complex.*

CUSTARD'S LAST STAND is a true family affair. Back in the late 1980s, Ray Julo and his brother Earl were looking to start up a family-owned business and asked their siblings and their spouses if they felt like joining in. The unanimous answer was yes, but the question remained about what type of establishment they would be running. After much research, which had them leaning towards opening up a flower shop, Ray happened to stop by TED DREWES FROZEN CUSTARD on a trip to St. Louis (see page 17). One taste brought on a custard epiphany and Ray realized that his calling was to bring high-quality custard to the Kansas City area. Fifteen years later, the Julos have built their own custard cult and have expanded to four company-run locations and two franchise shops.

All the locales are community oriented, featuring popular promotions such as the Custard's Last Stand Club. Run in conjunction with a local sports radio show, this promotion gives all club members discounts equal to the number of points the hometown Chiefs score that week. The shop sells Blue Bell premium ice cream, and flavored popcorn, but the homemade custard, made fresh throughout the day, is the main draw. This custard is best consumed in the form of one of their fabulous "papa-sized" concretes, a large order that contains concoctions so thick that one could use them to fill sidewalk cracks. Of these, my favorites were the **Libby's latte**, with hot fudge, Oreo, and cappuccino, and the **cherry smash**, combining cherries, chocolate chips, and mixed nuts.

JEFFERSON CITY

Central Dairy

ADDRESS 610 Madison St.
PHONE/WEB 573-635-6148
HOURS Sun 10a–6p, Mon–Sat 8a–6p
DIRECTIONS *The shop is attached to a dairy plant in the center of town right off Highway 50.*

A Jefferson City attraction second only to the nearby capitol building, CENTRAL DAIRY consists of both a large dairy plant and an ice cream parlor. Since the 1930s, the plant has produced and delivered dairy products for the surrounding region, adhering to the motto, "fresh as a Missouri morning." While its delivery business is still robust, the parlor draws customers to the listed address — a local hangout that just happens to serve some of the country's best ice cream. Throughout the day regulars file in and out, talking to the bevy of servers behind the counter and mingling with the plant's delivery drivers who punch in and out at the far end of the room. The shop's long counter showcases more than forty flavors on any given day, a staggering array that is a testament to its constant flow of customers. CENTRAL DAIRY is able to maintain fresh selections by serving more ice cream per dollar than I have ever witnessed. For only $1.50, you get three scoops that are so large I suspect they account for a week's worth of production for a normal cow. The **praline and cream** and the **butterscotch ripple** are the perfect blends of cream and sugary goodness, but be forewarned that $1.50 buys only one flavor, so make sure you really like your order or step it up to a mammoth two-flavored cone.

KANSAS CITY

Angie's Italian Ice and Frozen Custard

ADDRESS 1710 W. 39th St.
PHONE/WEB 816-931-2423
HOURS Sun 12a–9p, Mon–Sat 11a–10p; limited winter hours
DIRECTIONS *The shop is in the city center between Bell St. and Genesee St.*

Warning, if you are on a diet, do not walk within even a few blocks of ANGIE'S ITALIAN ICE AND FROZEN CUSTARD. The oversized ice cream cone perched high above the shop attracts customers from a great distance, and the red awning promoting the four basic food groups — ice cream, Italian ice, frozen custard, and hot dogs — will cause even the most diligent weight watcher to take a closer look. Once lured in, it is nearly impossible to restrain oneself from ordering a Chicago-style hot dog (with tomato, onion, mustard, sport peppers, celery salt, relish, and a pickle spear), some chili-cheese fries, and a **concrete** to wash it all down. For those with great willpower, ANGIE'S Italian ices, which are made fresh daily, are relatively healthy and worthy of their Philadelphia-style attribution. If you want a little more kick to your treat, try the **gelati**, an interesting combination of Italian ice and frozen custard layered together. These concoctions alternate between sweet and tart and are ANGIE'S most popular order.

Murray's Ice Creams & Cookies

ADDRESS 4120 Pennsylvania Ave.
PHONE/WEB 816-931-5646
HOURS Sun, Wed–Sat 12p–10p, closed Mon, Tue, and first week of December–first week of March
DIRECTIONS *The shop is set back in a cul-de-sac off Pennsylvania Ave. in the charming Westport district.*

During the nineteenth century the town of Westport was the place for settlers to stop and stock up on essential supplies for their trek west. Today, this historic neighborhood of red-brick buildings and tree-lined streets remains relatively unchanged and continues to be home to vital rations — the treats made at MURRAY'S ICE CREAMS & COOKIES. A display of just-baked cookies ambushes unsuspecting ice cream seekers as they walk in, immediately triggering internal calorie counters in an attempt to justify a double dose of goodies. For those who can pull their heads away from the ginger snaps layered with cinnamon frosting and the double-chocolate mounds, a selection of premium ice cream flavors awaits. The shop is constantly experimenting with recipes and has created over 200 flavors to date, of which sixteen are offered each day. While certain favorites, like the cream-cheese-based **chocolate flake fromage**, are always on hand, other flavors, such as the perfect **fudge raspberry rhapsody**, appear less frequently. In order to inform their clientele when a favorite flavor is being served, the shop allows customers to sign up and be called when certain offerings are available. Due to the time it takes to call each customer, MURRAY'S caps the calling list at sixty, so anyone not on the already full list for the holy **one drunk monk**, a Frangelico liquor base with chocolate espresso flakes and hazelnuts, must frequent the shop at the beginning of each month and pray that they arrive on the right day.

ST. LOUIS

Crown Candy Kitchen

ADDRESS 1401 St. Louis Ave.
PHONE/WEB 314-621-9650 / www.crowncandykitchen.com
HOURS Summer: Sun 12p–8p, Mon–Sat 10:30a–10p; Winter: Sun 12p–6p, Mon–Thu 10:30a–9p, Fri, Sat 10:30a–10p
DIRECTIONS *In the Old North St. Louis neighborhood, just north of downtown on the corner of St. Louis and N. 14th St.*

It does not get any more old-school than CROWN CANDY KITCHEN. The shop has been run by three generations of Karandzieff men at the same North St. Louis location since 1913, evolving from a St. Louis institution into a regional treasure. As the surrounding neighborhood slowly deteriorated over time, the Karandzieffs declined all offers to move, choosing to anchor the remaining community. This perseverance has paid off — today the neighborhood has reached up-and-coming status as people continue to come from throughout the city and beyond to eat their comfort food and taste homemade ice cream and sweets. More than likely you will be waited on by Tammy Siebels, the waitress half of the identical twin combo that has been working at the shop for over twenty-seven years. Her sister, Pam Mardirosian, works behind the scenes, but is just as crucial to the operation as she is part of the candy-making team. Get a BLT or chili dog to start; both are delicious and good sources of the essential grease to coat your digestive track before consuming a super-thick **chocolate banana malt.**

CHALLENGE:

Drink five 24-ounce malts in a half hour and they are on the house — the stomach pump, howev will cost you. Since the sh started keeping count in 1991, less than twenty people have been "successful."

EXTRA SCOOPS

Ice Cream Lore

Use of ice and snow for gastronomic purposes was first recorded in the cuneiform tablets of the Mesopotamians nearly three thousand years ago. These tablets reveal how wealthy citizens would use ice brought in from far-off locales to cool their drinks. By the time of the Roman Empire, chilled drink techniques had evolved into a culinary art, reaching a pinnacle during the reign of **Emperor Nero** (A.D. 37–68). Nero would command the swiftest runners in the land to transport snow from distant mountain tops to storage pits on his palace grounds. During his lavish banquets he would use the snow to pack a specially designed two-chambered glass, which transformed added fruit juices and wines into slushy elixirs. The fall of the Roman Empire brought an end to this practice in Europe, but recipes proliferated throughout China and the Middle East.

Legend has it that Marco Polo introduced a chilled milk drink to Venice upon his return home, but more than likely the reintroduction of frozen concoctions to Europe took place as a result of the Moors' conquest of Sicily in the ninth century. Along with agrarian reform and ceramic art, the Moors brought back the lost methods for freezing and flavoring ices. Native Sicilians quickly learned these methods and, utilizing Arabian and indigenous ingredients such as jasmine, almonds, saffron, and lemons, were able to create iced mixtures similar to today's sorbets. As the Italian peninsula once again became prosperous during the fifteenth century, these early ice cream artisans began a northern migration, slowly spreading their freezing techniques and secret recipes across the varied regions of Italy and eventually the rest of Europe.

Three Italian men in particular were instrumental in the evolution and dissemination of ice cream. A Tuscan chicken farmer of the early sixteenth century named Ruggeri became so well known for his **flavored ice sculptures** that he traveled with Caterina de' Medici as part of her bridal entourage to Marseilles. His ice sculpture for her wedding festivities quickly became the talk of Francis I's court and thus introduced the Italian ice tradition to France. Bernardo Buontalenti (ca. 1531–1608), was the epitome of a Renaissance man, working as an architect, designer, inventor, and ice cream pioneer. While many of his architectural projects still stand, his lasting achievement occurred during a moment of inspirational genius when he partially froze a mixture of milk, honey, egg yolk, and wine, hence creating the first frozen concoction to include both dairy and egg. Finally, ice cream parlors the world over owe a nod of gratitude to Francesco Procopio, a Sicilian fisherman of the late seventeenth century. Having migrated to Paris, Procopio opened up a café that sold granita (a slushy-like concoction), sorbet, and sherbet, making these treats available to the masses for the first time.

Centuries later, variants of these ice cream traditions would reach American shores, and it is here that this delicacy found creative individuals and a sweet-toothed audience that together took its production and consumption to new heights.

Ted Drewes Frozen Custard

ADDRESS 6726 Chippewa St.
PHONE/WEB 314-482-2652 / www.teddrewes.com
HOURS Open daily at 11a, closed January
DIRECTIONS *There are two locations in St. Louis; the Chippewa St. shop is west of the city center between Lansdowne Ave. and Plainview Ave.*

Like the Gateway Arch, TED DREWES FROZEN CUSTARD is a St. Louis icon that everyone should try to visit at least once in their lifetime. The Drewes family first started selling custard in 1929 and opened up the two current shops in 1931 and 1941. The latter of these is on historic Route 66, the artery of Americana, and is housed in, well, a house, because no ordinary retail space could accommodate the hordes of customers who flock to the shop. There are often over ten windows open to take orders, each with lines five deep of customers craving a taste of its unforgettable offerings. Custard is made in **vanilla** only, and many prefer to eat it in this pure, unadulterated form, but upon request ingredients are added to make their famous malts, sundaes, shakes, and **concretes**. The concretes are perhaps the most popular orders, as the shop is the originator of the drop-less version, which can be held upside down for minutes without the slightest movement. The **terramizzou** contains a secret blend of chocolate and pistachio nuts and the **Dutchman**, named after a local high school team, combines fresh roasted pecans, hot fudge, and butterscotch.

CHALLENGE:

*Order and eat a **southern delight** concrete, with praline pecans and butterscotch, during the holiday season and see if it helps you keep warm as you shop for one of the Drewes' Christmas trees.*

LINCOLN

University of Nebraska Dairy Store

ADDRESS 114 Food Industry Building
PHONE/WEB 402-472-2828 / www.dairystore.unl.edu
HOURS Summer: Sun 1p–10p, Mon–Sat 10a–10p; Fall & Spring: Sun 1p–8p, Mon–Sat 10a–8p; Winter: Sun 1p–6p, Mon–Sat 10a–6p
DIRECTIONS *On the East Campus off Holdrege St. between 37th St. and 38th St.*

THE DAIRY STORE has been a University of Nebraska fixture for over eighty years. Gone are the days when cows roamed what was then the university's farm and a nickel could buy all the milk you could drink, if you brought your own cup; but fear not, dairy science continues to be a hot subject on today's East Campus. Michelle Ziemann, the dairy operations research manager, has the luxury of access to over $100,000 worth of equipment and a never-ending workforce of eager students. Under her supervision the plant functions as a training and research center dedicated to producing top quality cheese and ice cream. Tours are offered to groups that make advance reservations, giving people a chance to see how the shop's goods are made and providing the opportunity to stand in a room full of nothing but block after block of Husker cheese — a Monterey Jack variation that, as one eager fan remarked, "tastes like victory." The student contribution makes for some interesting flavors, including the **purple oops**, the result of a mistaken addition of coconut flavoring in place of cotton candy. Other favorites that have alumni crowding the shop on game days are the **butter brickle**, with chunks of butter almond toffee, and the delicious **karamel kashew**.

Ted & Wally's

ADDRESS 1120 Jackson St.
PHONE/WEB 402-341-5827
HOURS Sun 12p–10:30p, Mon–Thu 11a–10:30p, Fri, Sat 11a–11:30p
DIRECTIONS *In the Old Market District between Jackson St. and Howard St.*

When you want ice cream with an edge, go to Omaha. Yes, you read that right; TED & WALLY'S, located in a refurbished service station in the heart of Omaha's rejuvenated Old Market District, is the hippest ice cream shop in the Midwest. The shop has long cultivated a following with the city's artistic community, as a venue for local indie bands and the occasional folk or country act, and as an installation space for visual artists. While these events are appreciated by customers, the main draw week after week is the homemade ice cream. The shop makes all of its ice cream using rock salt and two old-fashioned ice cream mixers that are displayed in front of the counter for all to see. Twelve flavors are always on hand, but the shop's artistic spirit carries over to this realm as well, so it is hard to predict which newly created flavors will be available at any given time. I was lucky enough to taste a sumptuous **Dutch chocolate** and an **amaretto custard** that left me a little tipsy, but if those are not on the list when you visit, let the shop's aura guide you to your own inspired choice.

Section 2

IOWA MINNESOTA WISCONSIN

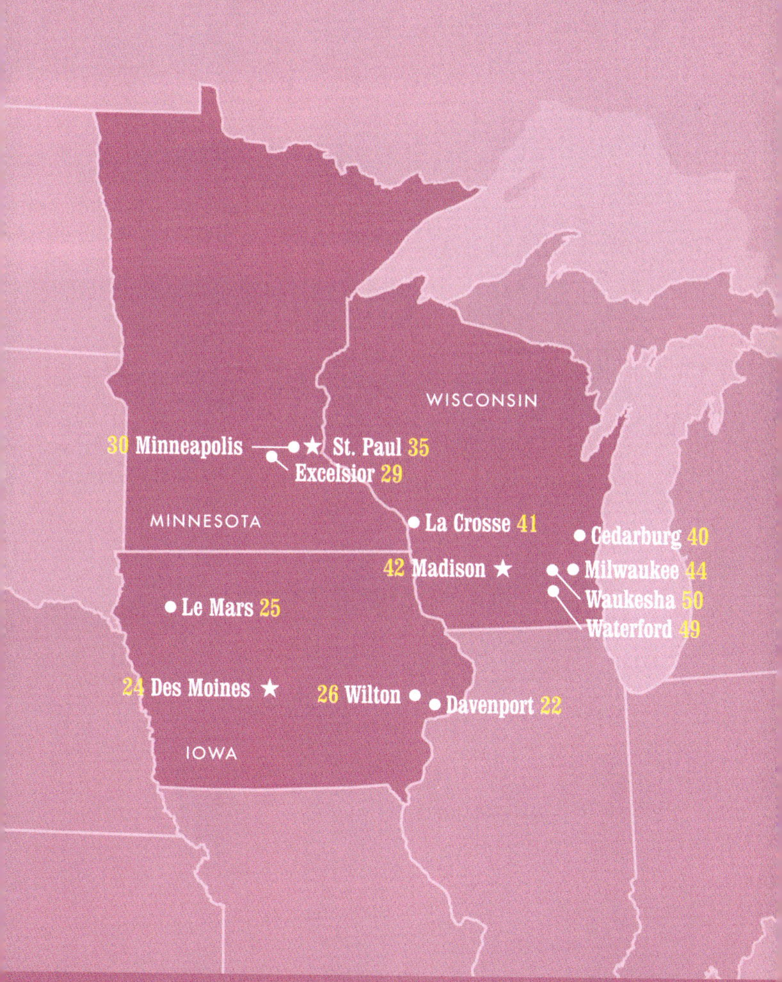

DAVENPORT / QUAD CITIES

Whitey's

ADDRESS 31230 W. Locust St.
PHONE/WEB 563-322-0828 / www.whiteysicecream.com
HOURS Sun–Thu 10a–10p, Fri, Sat 10a–11p
DIRECTIONS *Twelve locations throughout the Quad Cities, eastern Iowa, and western Illinois. The Locust St. shop is at the corner of Locust and Marquette streets.*

Baskin who? TCBW? Ben & Whitey's? These possibilities must run through the minds of Quad Cities residents when they venture out of WHITEY'S country. With a dozen shops, WHITEY'S has cornered the market on ice cream perfection in this lucky cluster of towns. To trace its origins one must go back to 1933, the year toe-headed Chester "Whitey" Lindgren opened the first shop. For the next twenty years he built a loyal following and in 1953 one of its first employees, Bob Tunberg, bought the business. Under the Tunbergs'

watch, WHITEY's truly became a family affair, with Bob and his wife, Norma, making ice cream during the day and selling it at night, and their young sons, Jeff and Jon, keeping the shop in mint condition by picking up any trash in the parking lot. In 1977 the company opened its second shop, beginning an expansionary phase that continues to this day. Jeff and Jon, who are now running the show, control a mini ice cream empire that includes a manufacturing facility that distributes WHITEY's flavors throughout a 150-mile radius in Illinois and Iowa. The secret to this success, besides serving premium ice cream, has been the company's squeaky clean image and commitment to customer service. Each shop is bright, spotless, and decked in red and white, with smiling, courteous servers always ready to please. The beauty is that this is not some 1950s nostalgia gimmick; it is just genuine Iowa friendliness. It goes without saying that the ice cream is fantastic, with standouts including **Whitey's delight**, a combination of French vanilla, Spanish peanuts, and chocolate chips, and the **Mississippi mud revel**, a mixture of Kona-coffee-flavored ice cream, fudge, and Oreo cookie bits.

CHALLENGE:

For those with
ra space in their belly,
*the **Boston**, a shake*
malt of your choice
ith a sundae on top!

DES MOINES

Bauder Pharmacy

ADDRESS 3802 Ingersoll Ave.
PHONE/WEB 515-255-1124
HOURS Sun 10a–2p, Mon–Fri 8:30a–4p, Sat 9a–4p
DIRECTIONS *A five-minute drive west of the capital at the intersection of Ingersoll and 38th St.*

Take two pints and call me in the morning. The continued success of BAUDER PHARMACY is a prime example of the power o good ice cream. In an age when most independent pharmacies have either been bought or driven out of business by regional consolidators, BAUDER PHARMACY has thrived, thanks in large part to the creamy concoctions made and sold on site. The sho was founded by pharmacist Carolyn Bauder back in the 1920s and in 1939 became a producer of prescriptions of a different kind, delicious ice cream. Her passion for this frozen delicacy was shared by the subsequent owner Charles Graziano, whose wife Corrine and children Mark and Kim continue to run the shop today. In many respects the shop functions as a typical pharmacy, with nearby residents stopping by throughout the day to pick up prescriptions, buy sundries, and peruse greeting cards. Even the charming soda counter and booths in the back do not do justice to the quality of the ice cream being served. The shop rotates its small selection of flavors to ensure that every batch you taste is as fresh as possible. Seasonal highlights are the **strawberry** and **cinnamon apple**, both of which contain chunks of just-picked fruit. If you are hungry for a meal try the homemade egg salad sandwich followed by their legendary **turtle sundae**, a mixture of ice cream, caramel, nuts, and hot fudge — a treat that is sure to cure all that ails you.

Blue Bunny

ADDRESS 26 Fifth Ave. NW
PHONE/WEB 712-546-4522 / www.bluebunny.com, www.wellsdairy.com
HOURS Sun 12p–10p, Mon–Sat 9a–10p
DIRECTIONS *In Northwestern Iowa, off Highway 75 between First and Plymouth St.*

Is this heaven? No it's Le Mars, Iowa. Any book on Midwest ice cream is not complete without a mention of this self-proclaimed Ice Cream Capital of the World®. It is here in Le Mars that the family-owned Wells' Dairy company produces more ice cream from one location, over 100 million gallons a year, than any other single business. For many years the company was content to distribute its BLUE BUNNY® line of products throughout the Midwest and beyond, but in the mid-1990s it decided to make Le Mars a destination for ice cream lovers the world over with the construction of the Ice Cream Capital of the World® Visitor Center. Over 15,000 visitors a year make a pilgrimage to this veritable ice cream compound to visit the ice cream parlor, gift shop, and museum. Further establishing the town's claim to ice cream fame is the Ice Cream Days Festival, held each year during Fourth of July week and featuring parades, band concerts, fireworks, and, need I even write, an ice cream social. All the ice cream sold at the parlor is made in three-gallon vats which ensure low air content and a premium taste. **Bunny tracks**, a vanilla base with fudge and peanut butter caramel ribbons, chocolate covered peanuts, and peanut butter-filled chocolate bunnies, is the biggest seller, but I was floored by the **homemade apple pie**, a blend of vanilla, caramel apple revel, spiced apples, and real pie pieces.

CHALLENGE:

*The **Goliath** is eight scoops of your choice piled high and topped with chocolate sauce, nuts, whipped cream, and a cherry. Surprisingly, the shop sells about four of these a day, a true sign that you are in dairy country.*

WILTON

Wilton Candy Kitchen

ADDRESS 310 Cedar St.
PHONE/WEB 563-732-2278
HOURS 7:30a–5p daily, closed from 12p–2p on Sun
DIRECTIONS *In downtown Wilton, south of Route 80, between Iowa City and Davenport.*

If you are disillusioned, sick of the monotony of shopping pods and vacation packages, jump in your car and head to Wilton, Iowa, population 2,829. Show up to the WILTON CANDY KITCHEN in the morning and take a seat at the counter with a handful of regulars and order up the special, a cup of coffee and some peanut butter toast. Talk to George Nopoulos and his wife, Thelma, and hear about the history of this "oldest ongoing ice cream parlor/soda fountain in the world," which is listed in the National Register of Historic Places. Listen to the story of how George's father, Gus, emigrated from Greece in 1907 and within three years bought the struggling shop. How despite onl knowing two words of English, "thank" and "you," he was able to keep the shop open 365 days a year through two wars and the Great Depression. Then ask about their meeting and hear of how after serving in WWII, George returned home to find Thelma working the counter and how he proposed in the offic of the CANDY KITCHEN in 1949. Take time to look around at the authentic walnut booths, the metal ceiling, and the marble soda fountain. Excuse yourself, drive the back roads of the surrounding farm country and return in the afternoon. Order up a dish of the ice cream — preferably **butter brickle** or **banana pineapple** — that has been made in-house since 191(and by George since 1946, or if you really want to indulge, a sundae topped off with homegrown crushed strawberries. Feel your soul being rejuvenated and consider yourself lucky to hav visited this remnant of the best small-town America has to offe Make plans to visit again next year … or sooner.

EXTRA SCOOPS

Not-so-plain Vanilla

The popularity of vanilla ice cream has led people to use vanilla to connote plain or boring, but in actuality the origins of this flavor could not be more exotic. Vanilla beans are the seed pods of a climbing orchid (Vanilla planifolia) that originally flourished in the wooded regions of Mexico. The Totonac Indians cultivated the flowers and developed a fermentation process that brought out the bean's natural flavors. Eventually the Aztec nation encroached upon the Totonac tribal lands and forced them to offer the beans, which the Aztecs used to flavor Xocoatl (their legendary chocolate drink), as ritual tributes to their emperors. The Spanish conquest of Mexico in the 16th century gave the bean its current name — vanilla means "small sheath" in Spanish — and introduced this flavoring to the Continent. Vanilla was an immediate hit, but supplies were limited and very expensive to purchase.

By the 19th century, the French and English decided to try to cultivate the orchid in their own lands by smuggling cuttings across the globe. At first these attempts were thwarted because the plants were not being pollinated by the tiny **melipona bee**, the carrier for the Mexican orchids. Since these bees were indigenous only to Mexico, another means needed to be found, and in 1841 a former slave named Edmond Albius developed a process for hand pollination on the French island of Reunion, off the southeastern tip of Madagascar. While some say this process had been perfected and kept secret by the Totonacs for centuries, Albius's discovery led to the first widespread cultivation of the bean on nearby islands as well as in Tahiti, India, Indonesia, and Uganda. Today the best Mexican vanilla beans are as good as any in the world, but it is generally accepted that bean-for-bean the best vanilla now comes out of Madagascar.

The labor intensive hand-pollination and **hand-picking** keeps vanilla pricey; after saffron and cardamom it is the third most expensive spice in the world. That has not, however, stopped Americans from annually consuming over half the world's supply, and the reason for this disproportional consumption is ice cream. According to the International Ice Cream Association, 29 percent of ice cream consumers cite vanilla as their preferred choice and 28 percent of all supermarket sales are vanilla, in each case far surpassing the next favorite flavors. Many mass-produced ice creams use synthetic vanilla, but the best ice cream parlors spend the extra money for the real thing. So the next time you are contemplating ordering a scoop of plain vanilla, ask if they use the real stuff; if they do, order away and take pleasure in the fact that you are making one of the most exotic choices possible.

EXCELSIOR

Adele's Frozen Custard

ADDRESS 800 Excelsior Blvd.
PHONE/WEB 952-470-0035
HOURS Summer: 11a–10:30p daily, closed January and February
DIRECTIONS *Twenty minutes west of Minneapolis, near the shores of Lake Minnetonka.*

Excelsior is a destination for Twin Cities residents looking to walk quaint streets, do some window shopping, and enjoy Lake Minnetonka, the largest body of water in the metro area. While boating, swimming, or ice fishing may be the main attraction for many, there is a devoted group of customers who view ADELE'S FROZEN CUSTARD as the real lure. Set on the outskirts of town in a stand-alone house, this shop is the only place busier than the marina on hot summer days — with customers routinely spilling out onto the outdoor porch and patio as well as lining up at the drive-thru window. The cause for this frenzy is their delectable frozen custard, which the shop openly asserts is "ice cream made better." This proclamation is true enough when applied to the **vanilla** and **chocolate** flavors that are always on hand, but is an understatement when discussing the served-twice-a-month **chocolate raspberry truffle**, a momentous taste experience.

MINNEAPOLIS

Caruso's Gelato Café

ADDRESS 3001 Hennepin Ave. S.
PHONE/WEB 612-822-2629
HOURS Sun 11a–8p, Mon–Thu 11a–10p, Fri, Sat 11a–11p
DIRECTIONS *On the ground floor of Calhoun Square in Minneapolis' Uptown district.*

Cy Decosse had his first bite of gelato during his stay in Florence as a Fulbright Scholar in the 1950s. Over the next half century he accomplished many things, including building a successful publishing house that bore his name, but gelato always remained on his brain. Having sold his publishing business in the early 1990s, he began the process of building an authentic Italian gelateria in his native Minneapolis. To ensure that the shop would emit a true gelateria ambiance, he bought and imported a gelato display case, devised a menu that offers panini (hot, pressed Italian sandwiches), and searched for the right coffee blends in order to serve genuine espressos and cappuccinos. The preparation was even more intense concerning the shop's gelato. First, CARUSO'S hired a recipe developer who had spent much of her career developing foods for Pillsbury. Then, in order to get the gelato just right, Mr. Decosse tapped a relationship he had been cultivating for fifty years, and had employees from the Florentine gelateria PERCHÉ NO? (Why not?) flown to Minneapolis to instruct his team in the art of gelato making. After years of groundwork, the shop opened in 2001 and has been a booming success. Crowds line up at night to taste the creamy **pistachio**, smooth **banana**, and decadent **dark chocolate**. While a stroll over the Ponte Vecchio may not be possible, Minnesotans are happy to have this little piece of authentic Italy in their own backyard.

Crema Café / Sonny's Ice Cream

ADDRESS 3403 Lyndale Ave. S.
PHONE/WEB 612-824-3868
HOURS Sun 10a–10p, Tue–Fri 11a–10p, Sat 10a–12a
DIRECTIONS *In South Minneapolis, on the corner of Lyndale Ave. S. and 34th St.*

The roots of CREMA CAFÉ can be traced back to Sonny Siron, who, after serving in World War II, returned home to open a malt shop, offering hamburgers and homemade ice cream from the ground floor of his Lyndale Avenue residence. The shop eventually closed, but Sonny and his son, Ron, the current co-owner, continued to make Sonny's ice cream for local restaurants and markets. This wholesale business was profitable, but the monotony of producing batch after batch of vanilla and chocolate had begun to wear on Ron, who had been making ice cream with his dad since the age of ten. At about this same time in the early 1990s, Carrie Gustafson, the other current co-owner, was traveling in Italy, whereupon she visited VIVOLI, the renowned Florentine gelateria. One taste of their *riso* (rice) gelato brought on an ice cream epiphany, and Carrie knew she had found her calling. Determined to open an ice cream shop in her native Minneapolis, she tracked down Sonny's ice cream duo, and after much persuading, convinced Ron to let her work for them at no charge. Within two years, her creativity had seeped its way into Ron's soul, and together they set about opening CREMA CAFÉ, transforming their previously drab building into an Italian paradise. The result is a sophisticated ice cream shop that has enough charm to make visitors think they have entered a Venetian wine bar. This is fitting because Carrie and Ron approach making ice cream and sorbet the same way vintners go about making a fine wine, carefully testing each new creation to ensure that it contains layers of taste. Their commitment is evident in each flavor, including the signature **crema**, which involves a seventy-two-hour coffee bean infusion process, the unbeatable **ultimate chocolate**, for which the pair tested over

CONTINUED >

CREMA / SONNY'S CONTINUED

twenty-five recipes before choosing a blend of three different chocolates, and the **cucumber sorbet**, containing pinot grigio and infused mint. This remarkable ice cream is also available at local supermarkets and gourmet stores as far away as Chicago, under the brand names Sonny's (which after six hundred hours of work has achieved the status of certified organic) and Ahana (featuring the Company's Asian blends). Sonny himself, however, is available only to those visiting the shop — where he continues to live.

The Pumphouse Creamery

ADDRESS 4754 Chicago Ave. S.
PHONE/WEB 612-825-2021 / www.pumphousecreamery.com
HOURS 12p–10p daily, closed December to mid-March
DIRECTIONS *In South Minneapolis, between 47th and 48th streets.*

The next time you feel like witnessing a true labor of love, head to THE PUMPHOUSE CREAMERY. Barb Zapzalka, the owner of the shop, is not a typical business owner concerned with the bottom line and harboring dreams of expansion and ensuing riches. Instead, she is an artisan, whose works can be ordered and devoured rather than hung on a wall and gazed upon. Barb grew up on a farm in central Minnesota, making hand-cranked ice cream several times a year near the pump house referenced in the shop's name. After beginning her career as a systems analyst she realized that the old adage about not being able to take the farm out of the girl was correct, and decided to set off on her own and start up a business that would be true to her roots. Her lifelong passion for ice cream made the choice of business easy, and in May 2003 the PUMPHOUSE opened its doors to the public. The shop uses only organic milk and cream bought from local farmers, and purchases ingredients from co-ops and distributors who sell only the finest produce, herbs, and extracts. The results are delectable flavors including the deceptively flavorful **chocolate banana** and an **oatmeal cookie** that not only contains large cookie pieces from a nearby bakery, but also happened to induce my wife's labor — no joke. Those looking to try something new should taste the **grapefruit** sorbet or the **kulfi**, an Indian ice cream that contains pistachios, cardamom, and rosewater. Also on hand are thirty-two bottled sodas, including eleven root beer varieties from microbreweries across the country.

Sebastian Joe's Ice Cream Café

ADDRESS 1007 W. Franklin Ave.
PHONE/WEB 612-870-0065
HOURS Sun–Thu 7a–11p, Fri, Sat 7a–12a
DIRECTIONS *In the Lowry Hill/Uptown district, on the corner of Franklin and Hennepin avenues. Another location is in the Linden Hills district.*

SEBASTIAN JOE'S is owned by three Pellizer brothers and named in honor of their Italian immigrant grandfather, whose real name was converted to Joe on his first day of work in America by a foreman unwilling to pronounce Sebastiano. The shop, which opened in 1985, maintains an elegant style and hip ambiance worthy of the owners' Italian heritage, with marble counters, two indoor seating areas, outdoor tables that are always packed during nice weather, and a selection of over twenty European coffee blends. Solidifying it as a hot spot are two iMacs available for customers to use to surf the Net, a WiFi system allowing anyone with a laptop and wireless modem to find a comfy chair and log on, and, for those who prefer more traditional means of getting their information, a selection of newspapers and magazines. If it sounds idyllic, wait until you try the ice cream. Everything is made with the utmost care, from the **hand-dipped cones** — try the Butterfinger or coconut — to the **B-RRR bars**, Oreo ice cream smothered in dark chocolate on a stick. The shop continually rotates a selection of inventive flavors of which I enjoyed the chocolate-based **praline home companion** and the ever-popular **raspberry chocolate chip**.

CHALLENGE:

*The shop runs a winter-time offer that gives customers a discount for every degree below freezing the outside temperature reaches for the day. Take advantage of this and order the mammoth **Joe's banana boat** sundae, three large scoops of your choice, a banana, hot caramel or hot fudge, a topping, and whipped cream. On a cold Minneapolis night you could save big bucks — just don't try to eat it outside.*

SAINT PAUL

Grand Ole Creamery

ADDRESS 750 Grand Ave.
PHONE/WEB 651-293-1655
HOURS Summer: Sun–Thu 11a–11p, Fri, Sat 11a–12a
DIRECTIONS *In the western part of St. Paul, between Victoria St. and Dale St.*

For twenty years, the GRAND OLE CREAMERY, set in the middle of historic Grand Avenue, has been St. Paul's ice cream parlor of choice. While different ice cream trends, from frozen yogurt to mix-ins, have come and gone and new competitors have sprouted up, the CREAMERY has continued to pack in customers by producing great ice cream. The shop earned a top-ten in the nation ranking by citysearch.com, is routinely named one of the best parlors in the Twin Cities, and has won numerous "Grandest of the Grand" awards. Eight waffle irons constantly churn out fresh waffle cones and waffle cups, emitting an enticing aroma that travels down the block in the process. A second room holds additional seating, a jukebox, a couple of video games (including an old-school Ms. Pacman), and a separate counter that serves cones, cups, and pints when business reaches a frenzy on warm summer nights. Everything is delicious and made on the premises, but if I had to order just one cone I would get the **chocolate malt banana**, which is addictive at first bite, topped off with a scoop of their refreshing **strawberry**.

Izzy's Ice Cream Café

ADDRESS 2034 Marshall Ave.
PHONE/WEB 651-603-1458 / www.izzysicecream.com
HOURS Sun 12p–9p, Mon–Thu 12p–10p, Fri, Sat 12p–10:30p, closed late-December–April
DIRECTIONS *On the western edge of St. Paul, a minute from the Cretin/Vandalia I-94 exit. Another shop is in the Medical Arts building in downtown Minneapolis.*

In five short years IZZY'S ICE CREAM CAFÉ has grown from a fledgling shop into a multi-location business that was named the 2004 Ice Cream Store of the Year by the Ice Cream University. This impressive achievement is a testament to the creativity and passion of husband-and-wife owners Jeff Sommers and Lara Hammel. Their passion is no more evident than in the community events the shop holds, including a four-square tournament and the People's Flavor Awards, an annual contest that invites any and all to sample a selection of flavors that were submitted by customers and produced by IZZY'S. For creative marketing, one need not look beyond the legendary izzy, a cure for those who, like Sommers, suffer from the "Minnesota Nice" syndrome — feeling that it is too forward and even borderline decadent to ask for taste samples before ordering a cone. The **izzy**, his ingenious solution, augments the shop's already liberal tasting policy by giving customers a complimentary quarter scoop, allowing them to have both their favorite flavor and try something new. Thank the ice cream gods for that extra option, because there are a plethora of flavors you will want to sample, including the **St. Paul hotel**, packed with almonds and home-made hot fudge, the **Irish moxie**, and the transcontinental and extremely tasty **Norwegian chai**, an Asian chai tea blend mixed with Norwegian cardamom toast.

CHALLENGE: *The double scoop* ***Izzabella*** *consists of a homemade waffle cone dipped in chocolate rolled in imported Marcona almon filled with two scoops of your cho and topped with fresh whipped cr and an Obläten wafer. This refin treat even includes a Marcona alm bon bon at the bottom of the cone prevent dripping, and a fortune wr by a local poet, whose words o wisdom in my case were fitting "two scoops is better than one.*

EXTRA SCOOPS

The Great Cone Controversy

The debate surrounding the invention of the ice cream cone is over a century old and is not likely to ever be fully resolved. While before the turn of the twentieth century metal and paper cones were used in France and waffle cones were employed in Germany, the introduction of cones to the United States is believed to have come via a moment of inspiration rather than as an overseas import. As early as 1896 an Italian immigrant named Italo Marchiony had begun making ice cream cone prototypes, and in 1903 he applied for a patent for an ice cream cup mold. This patent has led some to believe that Marchiony was the rightful inventor of the American cone, but closer inspection shows that the patent was for edible cups with handles, not cones at all. Instead, the general consensus is that the cone was introduced at the 1904 St. Louis World's Fair. This, however, is where the consensus ends.

Several different men lay claim to the World's Fair cone phenomenon, each with a story as unusual as the next. Charles Menches, a successful vendor who made a living selling confections at fairs, is linked to a couple of cone stories. The most bizarre account involves his purchase of a bouquet of flowers and an ice cream sandwich for a lady he was accompanying. This enterprising woman is then remembered as having rolled the two wafers from the sandwich into separate cones, one to serve as a vase for the flowers and one for the ice cream! Another man, a Lebanese immigrant named Abe Doumar, is said to have suggested to a waffle maker at the fair that he make waffle cones for the

nearby ice cream sellers, following his countrymen's tradition of forming cones with pita bread to hold jam. The waffle maker was so grateful for the money-making tip that he gave Abe a waffle iron, which he used to start up his own cone business.

The most credible story, however, involves a Syrian immigrant named Ernest Hamwi. Hamwi had originally set up shop at the fair as a purveyor of zalabia, a type of waffle traditionally topped with sugar. Serendipitously, his booth was located next to one of the fair's many ice cream stands, and it was not long before customers began buying his waffles and topping them with his neighbor's ice cream. Hamwi realized the waffles made ice cream a portable treat, ideal for strolling and taking in the nearby attractions, and he quickly set about designing a better transport medium. After a few failed attempts, Hamwi instructed his workers to role the waffles into a funnel shape, thus resulting in the World's Fair cornucopia. The cornucopia, or cone, was an immediate hit and led to the creation of the Cornucopia Cone Company, for which Hamwi worked as a promoter, and eventually the establishment of the Missouri Cone Company, which Hamwi owned.

After the World's Fair, cones and cone ovens became readily available and soon molded cones began appearing, marking the first of many cone variations to appeal to the public. Today you can choose among waffle, wafer, sugar, and even pretzel varieties, and at many shops you can select from an array of coatings, including chocolate, sprinkles, coconut, and crushed candy bars. While the controversy surrounding the invention of the cone may never be settled, there is no disputing that over the past century the cone has risen from its humble beginning to a prized position within America's culinary hierarchy.

REFERENCE: *CHOCOLATE, STRAWBERRY AND VANILLA: A HISTORY OF AMERICAN ICE CREAM,* ANNE COOPER FUNDERBURG (BOWLING GREEN UNIVERSITY POPULAR PRESS, 1995)

CEDARBURG

The Chocolate Factory

ADDRESS W62 N577 Washington Ave.
PHONE/WEB 262-377-8877 / www.subsandicecream.com
HOURS Sun–Thu 11a–9p, Fri, Sat 11a–10p
DIRECTIONS *Thirty minutes north of Milwaukee; seven other shops are located throughout the area.*

Cedarburg's charming Washington Avenue has remained virtually unchanged over the past century and for that reason is listed in the National Register of Historic Places. Anchoring this main street is the original site of THE CHOCOLATE FACTORY, a shop that curiously enough does not serve chocolate, but rather specializes in subs and ice cream. This dual function ensures that the shop remains busy all year, with subs drawing crowds in the dead of winter, and ice cream packing them in during the summer. THE CHOCOLATE FACTORY is the sole outlet for Blommer's ice cream, a local producer since the 1920s. This ice cream is superb, with a wide selection of unusual flavors including the **Swiss chocolate mint** and the **roasted pistachio**. While this shop stands on its own, I must admit that I have a special connection, for I am close to the Washington, D.C. branch of the Blommer clan — all of whom can blackmail me with a childhood picture of Selden, the youngest Blommer daughter, and myself in matching tutus. For those who also crave a non–ice cream treat, try one of the caramel apples from AMY'S CANDY KITCHEN, conveniently located right next door.

CHALLENGE:

*Try the "double dare flavor of the month," with past entries including the savory **smoky bacon** and the potent **bloody Mary.***

LA CROSSE

The Sweet Shop

ADDRESS 1113 Caledonia St.
PHONE/WEB 608-784-7724
HOURS Sun 12p–5p, Mon–Sat 9a–5p
DIRECTIONS *One block east of the town's main drag, Rose St.*

La Crosse, nestled in among the bluffs and bald eagles of this section of the Mississippi, is a pleasant river town and favorite day trip for residents of the upper Midwest. Activities such as river cruises and hikes to scenic overlooks are recommended, but those in the know are aware that a trip to The Sweet Shop is obligatory. The shop is a mixture of old and new, selling homemade ice cream and chocolates as well as giant Bart Simpson Pez dispensers. The selection of flavors includes the cult favorite **blue moon**, but the real find here is the **chocolate marsh**. This terrific flavor mixes chocolate ice cream with homemade marshmallow sauce, creating a unique consistency in which the ice cream and marshmallows become one. Good **marshmallow sauce** is hard to find these days, so I suggest ordering a **marshmallow sundae** to get your fill. Other sundaes are each named after local high schools, and school spirit dictates orders — an Onalaska student would never purchase an Aquinas High sundae. Before you leave, make sure to pick up one of the caramel suckers; the large version is big enough to sustain a sweet tooth for a trip down the Ol' Miss.

MADISON

Babcock Hall Dairy Store (www.icecreamsource.com)

ADDRESS 1605 Linden Dr.
PHONE/WEB 608-262-3045 / www.wisc.edu/foodsci/store
HOURS Mon–Fri 9:30a–5:30p, Sat 10a–1:30p, closed Sun
DIRECTIONS *In Babcock Hall on the UW Madison campus.*

In this state where cheese curds roam free and sour cream flows from the tap, it is fitting that the University of Wisconsin at Madison has the oldest dairy school in the country, dating back to 1891. Though research and instruction have always been its main goals, the school also produces a range of dairy products for students and the general public. Using the ubiquitous Wisconsin Badger mascot as its logo, the BABCOCK HALL DAIRY STORE offers a dizzying array of cheeses, including eight different types of cheddar. While the cheeses are popular, the main draw is the homemade ice cream, all of which is produced by students on site. Twelve regular flavors are always on hand, including the addictive **coffee and truffles**, as well as selections of monthly featured flavors that range from the **honey graham cracker**, vanilla with Wisconsin wildflower honey and graham cracker pieces, to the alumni favorite, **orange custard chocolate chip**. Besides the Babcock Hall location, the ice cream is sold at other school cafeterias and nonaffiliated shops throughout town — the best of which is the dual-purpose MONONA BAIT AND ICE CREAM, selling everything anybody could want for a day on the lake.

Michael's Frozen Custard

ADDRESS 2531 Monroe St.
PHONE/WEB 608-231-3500 / www.ilovemichaels.com
HOURS Sun–Thu 11a–10:30p, Fri, Sat 11a–11p
DIRECTIONS *Five minutes south of the main campus; two other locations in Madison and one in Verona.*

MICHAEL'S FROZEN CUSTARD is the undisputed king of custard in Madison, having been named the city's best every year since its opening in 1986. This success was built on adherence to the motto, "bigger burgers, better custard," and has earned it a four-shop minimonopoly within this region of custard-crazed Wisconsin. The original shop is set up in a converted gas station, with seats replacing pumps, grease found on grills rather than cars, and custard the new fuel of choice. To deal with the summertime rush, the shop offers both an indoor and a walk-up express window, allowing customers ample opportunity to order. In addition to the usual options, these loyal patrons line up for tastes of the daily flavor specials, with favorites including the **mint brownie** and the **blueberries 'n' cream**.

CHALLENGE:

If you happen to visit on April Fool's Day be sure to try the fool's favorites, with past flavors including ***broccoli chip*** *and* ***worms 'n dirt.***

MILWAUKEE & VICINITY

Gilles Frozen Custard

ADDRESS 7515 W. Bluemound Rd.
PHONE/WEB 414-453-4875 / www.gillesfrozencustard.com
HOURS Sun–Thu 10:30a–10:30p, Fri, Sat 10:30a–11p
DIRECTIONS *Ten to fifteen minutes west of the city center.*

Milwaukee's oldest custard stand is also one of its best. Since 1938, Gilles Frozen Custard has been dishing creamy, smooth custard and has in the process built a devoted following. Gilles does not have the neon flash of Leon's or the futuristic efficiency of Kopp's, but it does have a comfortable feel that can only be achieved with years of good service. Anytime you can walk into a shop and order "a gillieburger, a bananarama, and one of those things," and have it make perfect sense, you know you are in for a treat. While locals need no help translating, let me help the uninitiated understand. The gillieburger is a mild barbecue beef sandwich, one of the many noncustard selections that have been drawing in Major League Baseball Commissioner Bud Selig on a daily basis for over thirty years (truth be told, he is a hot dog and soda guy). The **bananarama**, vanilla custard served with bananas, strawberries, pineapple, marshmallow, chocolate jimmies, chopped nuts, and cherries, is one of the shop's fancy sundaes. Any and all of these treats are worth the trip, but the shop's signature **those things**, a peanut butter cookie encased in vanilla custard and wrapped in milk chocolate, is the item that has me counting the days until my next Gilles visit.

CHALLENGE:

***The zombie sundae**, a modified bananarama with an extra scoop of custard and the welcome additions of hot fudge and pecans, is truly trance-enhancing.*

Kopp's Frozen Custard

ADDRESS 5373 N. Port Washington Rd., Glendale
PHONE/WEB 414-961-3288 / www.kopps.com
HOURS 10:30a–11p daily
DIRECTIONS *In Glendale, fifteen minutes north of Milwaukee city center; additional locations in Brookfield and Greenfield.*

If eating Kopp's butter burgers and frozen custard is wrong, I don't want to be right. In a city where cream is king, Kopp's has risen above its competitors and achieved national recognition for what is generally considered the world's best custard. It is almost as if the shop operates in the not-too-distant future, where custard is richer and burgers are larger. The elegant sign at the Glendale location draws passersbys to what from the outside looks like a highway rest stop. Inside there is an astounding number of shiny stainless steel custard machines, and when you add in the myriad of workers scurrying to and fro and the nine separate registers on hand to deal with the inevitable rushes, one gets the sense of having entered a custard mission control. Do not treat your first visit to Kopp's as any ordinary indulgence; rather think of it more as a pilgrimage. Dieting and, better yet, fasting before you go will allow you to truly enjoy all the shop has to offer. Begin with a small order of **vanilla** to taste what frozen custard is supposed to be. Follow that up with a double butter burger, enough meat for a family of five, but consumed regularly by diehards. Finish with a large serving of the rotating flavor of the day, and hope that your visit coincides with the **midnight chocolate cake**, with chocolate truffle pieces, thick fudge, and dark chocolate custard, or the **macadamia nut**, which, as they tell you, is "too expensive for us to make, so don't buy it, we lose money!"

EXTRA SCOOPS

King Custard

Trying to order ice cream in Wisconsin is similar to the scene in the *Simpsons* episode of "Bart vs. Australia" where, while visiting a local pub, Marge asks for a cup of coffee and the bartender quickly responds, "beer it is." Ice cream is not impossible to find, but frozen custard is far and away the preferred choice of this dairy-loving state. A by-state examination of the indispensable Web site custardlist.com, which, among other things, allows users to view the flavor of the day at over 250 shops, reveals that over 50 percent of the country's custard stands are in Wisconsin. While this percentage may be slightly high — custardlist.com only lists shops that have chosen to participate — the fact remains that custard is in **Wisconsin's dairy pantheon**, holding as prized a place as sour cream, cheese curds, and the all powerful cheddar cheese.

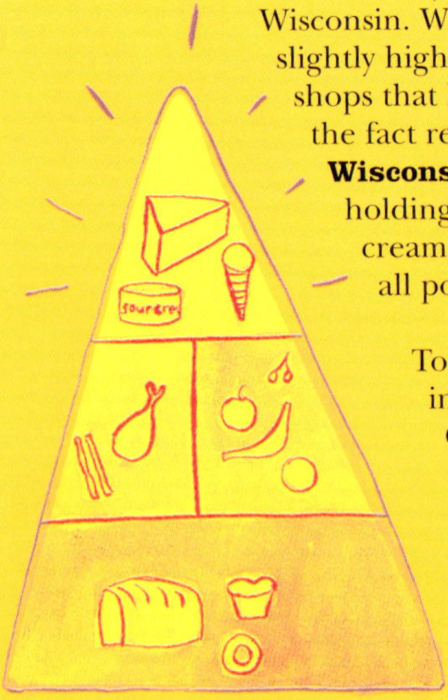

To trace the roots of this custard infatuation one must begin in Coney Island in 1919. Legend has it that on this date a Coney Island ice cream vendor added egg to his flavors in order to prevent them from melting too quickly. The unintended result was a new, super premium ice cream that, because of the egg mixture, could be served at a higher temperature and could contain less air. Combined, these two benefits prevented taste buds from becoming numbed, a common occurrence in standard ice cream, and created a heavier, smoother end product. Coney Island visitors devoured this new marvel, and it was not long before frozen custard had spread to beach resorts throughout the East Coast. When thousands of Midwesterners tasted frozen custard for the first time at the 1933 Chicago World's Fair, the custard craze truly began. Seduced by its creamy, dense consistency and super-rich flavor, these fair-goers spread the gospel of custard, and in the ensuing years frozen custard stands began to pop up throughout the region.

Nowhere did frozen custard take a greater hold than in Milwaukee, today's acknowledged "Custard Capital of the World." While I have listed what I believe to be the three best custard stands in town, there are a multitude of other shops that would be institutions in any other city. You could spend a week touring the various stands in and around Milwaukee, eating giant butter burgers and perfecting your custard palate. While your waistline would probably expand a tad, you would no doubt reach the custard nirvana so commonly experienced by the residents of "cream city."

Leon's Frozen Custard

ADDRESS 3131 S. 27th St.
PHONE/WEB 414-383-1784
HOURS 11a–12a daily
DIRECTIONS *Just south of city center, on the corner of W. Oklahoma Ave. and S. 27th St.*

Founded in 1942 and last renovated in 1955, LEON'S FROZEN CUSTARD is an authentic remnant of the car-hop craze and, thanks to the TV show *Happy Days*, one of Milwaukee's most recognizable landmarks. While Al's Diner of Fonzie fame is not an exact replica of LEON'S, the resemblance is close enough to back up the claim that it was modeled after it. Run by the Schneider family since its opening, the shop has seen no need to change with the times, and while service at your car is no longer offered, the setting is still enough to stir up memories of convertibles with long fins, greasers on bikes, and beehive hairdos. First timers should make sure to visit LEON'S at night, when the shop is awash in bright neon and the parking lot is packed. While the lights draw people in, it is the custard that keeps them coming back. In addition to their top-rate **vanilla** and **chocolate**, LEON'S always offers its legendary **butter pecan** as well as great flavors of the day, including a tart **raspberry** and a superb **cinnamon**.

WATERFORD

Uncle Harry's Frozen Custard and Ice Cream

ADDRESS 100 S. Jefferson St.
PHONE/WEB 262-534-4757
HOURS Seasonal, please call for hours
DIRECTIONS *Thirty minutes south of Milwaukee.*

Custard and ice cream stands are plentiful in Wisconsin, so when people drive thirty minutes out of their way to visit a particular shop, passing several options in the process, the product is bound to be memorable. Such is the case with UNCLE HARRY'S of Waterford, luring in customers, including regulars from twenty-minutes-away Racine, from throughout the area. When the shop was founded in 1985 by Harry Dombrowski, it functioned primarily as a gas station that happened to serve frozen custard. By 1992 its edible offerings had become so popular that it was converted into a custard shop. Today, under the watchful eye of its fourth owners Beth and Michael Artery, UNCLE HARRY'S bears little resemblance to a gas station. Charming features, such as little eating nooks and an exterior window that allows customers to watch the manufacturing process, create a family-friendly ambiance. Typically a shop specializes in frozen custard or ice cream, and never the twain shall meet, but UNCLE HARRY'S bucks this trend by selling over seventy flavors of frozen custard, ice cream, Italian ice, nonfat frozen yogurt, and fat-free sugar-free yogurt. Seventeen of these flavors have won the Wisconsin Seal of Excellence at the Wisconsin State Fair, including a splendid **strawberry** frozen custard and a **toasted pecan fudge** old-fashioned ice cream that will drop you to your knees in appreciation.

WAUKESHA

Divino Gelato Cafe

ADDRESS 227 W. Main St.
PHONE/WEB 262-446-9490 / www.divinogelatocafe.com
HOURS Sun, Sat 1p–9p, Mon–Fri 11a–9p
DIRECTIONS *In the center of historic Waukesha.*

In the summer of 2002 Judi Sottile journeyed to Italy during an unusually hot stretch of weather, with temperatures hovering at 100 degrees. Rather than search for air-conditioning, Judi took to the streets and toured the country using her new-found weapon, gelato. Two to three times a day she would stop by a gelateria and order a few scoops of Italy's best dessert. By the end of the trip she had become so attached to gelato that she decided to open up a gelateria in her native Wisconsin, and in June of 2003 DIVINO GELATO CAFE opened its doors. As noted several times in this guide, Wisconsin is frozen custard country, so at first the shop had to educate customers about the benefits of this lower in fat, yet extremely flavorful version of ice cream. Within a short time, however, DIVINO established a loyal customer base that now downs gelato on a regular basis. In fact, on the occasions when DIVINO is closed, Judi has to alert people well ahead of time so they make sure to buy some pints to tide them over till she re-opens — which is usually within twenty-four hours. All the flavors are listed in Italian and English, and Italian staples, such as the **fruto di bosco** (mixed berry) and **pistacchio**, are always on hand. DIVINO also puts its own twist on a few classics, with the **raspberry crema**, which uses a cream base rather than a water/juice base, and **passion fruit** among the best-selling flavors.

EXTRA SCOOPS

Finding Great Ice Cream

Loyalty is a noble character trait. I admire people who stand by their friends even when they do something inexplicable like grow a mullet or streak at a ballgame. I think couples that remain monogamous should get a card that allows them to cut in line in front of adulterers at grocery stores, movie theaters, and airports. I respect loyal people, but when it comes to your relationship with your favorite ice cream shop, I think you should be unfaithful. You do not eat sandwiches from only one deli or pies from only one pizzeria, so why should you frequent only one ice cream shop? Perhaps the reason is that ice cream is just so tasty that people cannot imagine better flavors served anywhere other than their favorite shop. Well, I agree, ice cream is tasty, but there are major and subtle differences amongst shops and these differences lead to a wide variety of interesting ambiances and flavors. So go ahead, cheat on your local parlor, it will still be there the next time you need a scoop and **your ice cream affair** will make your old stand-by seem that much more delicious. For those who have been out of the ice cream dating scene for a while, here are some tips to finding a worthy shop.

1. Research. We have done most of this work for you, but there are undoubtedly some good Midwestern parlors that we have missed. Additionally, we hope that many of you will make ice cream expeditions part of your itinerary when traveling outside the Midwest. Before you begin an ice cream quest, ask friends about their favorites, perform a web search, or better yet, e-mail us for a suggestion.

2. Be independent. Forego the national chains; they are focused on the bottom line, not your palate. Whose ice cream would you prefer, an "executive chef's" made at a plant in another state or a local owner's/operator's who prepared his or her ice cream fresh that morning?

3. Follow the cone. Be willing to let good ice cream find you. If you are walking down an unfamiliar street and happen to see a noticeable trend of people carrying cones, drop what you are doing and follow that trail of cones to its source.

4. Breathe in. If you can smell an ice cream parlor before you see it, proceed through its doors. The aroma of freshly baked waffle cones is one of life's small pleasures, and shops that care enough to bake cones on a regular basis are near locks to serve great ice cream.

5. Observe. Look for telltale signs such as long lines, reviews posted on the wall, or a general sense of community with its customers. Bulletin boards of kids with cones or quirky logos/mantras are good; fluorescent lights or overly sterile environments are bad.

6. Inquire. Ask if they make the ice cream on-site or nearby. If you do not get a straight answer then there is a good chance that the ice cream is not worth your time.

7. Inspect. Check to see if the ice cream looks appetizing. Good ice cream is consistent in appearance, but not necessarily pretty. If colors seem too bright or unnatural there is a good chance artificial flavorings and/or colorings have been added. A good benchmark is banana: if it is yellow, then pass, if it has a grayish hue, then order away.

8. Sample. Any shop worth a lick will let you try a multitude of flavors before you order. Do not think of it as an imposition — it is your duty to sample and find the cone that is just right for you.

9. Savor the Flavors. Enjoy your cone, you deserve it.

Section 3

ILLINOIS INDIANA

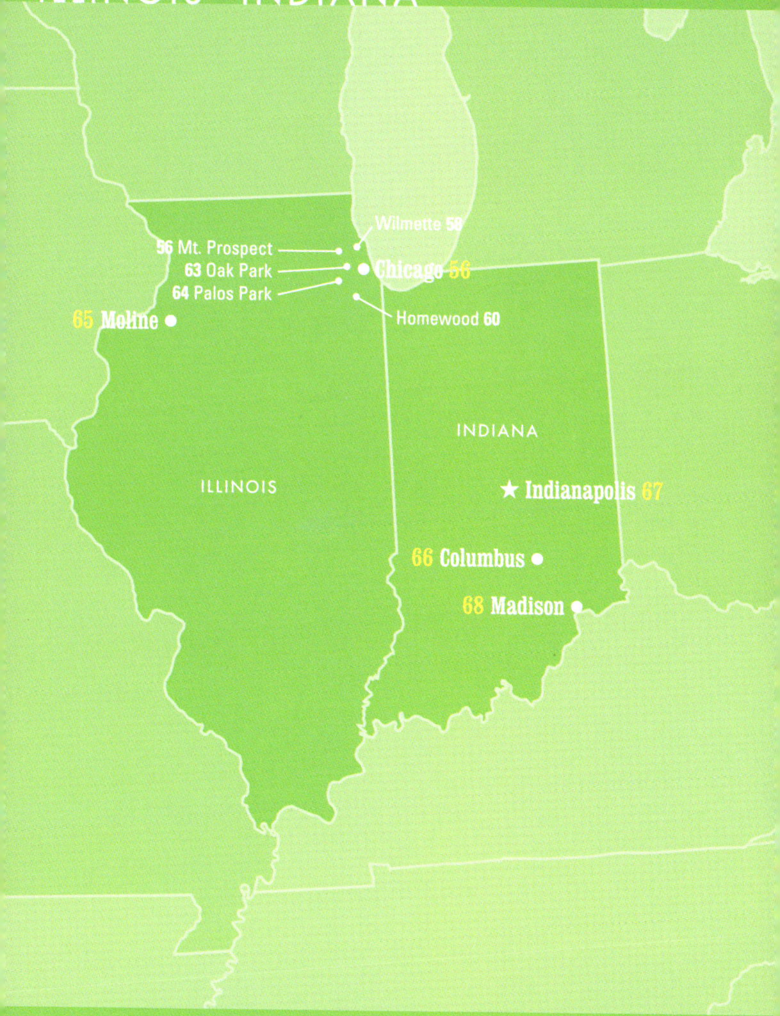

CHICAGO & VICINITY

Capannari Ice Cream

ADDRESS 10 S. Pine St., Mt. Prospect
PHONE/WEB 847-392-2277 / www.capannaris.com
HOURS Sun–Thu 12p–10p, Fri, Sat 12p–11p, closed October 30–March 15 (during this time the space converts into an art gallery/tea room and prepackaged pints are available for purchase)
DIRECTIONS *Forty minutes northwest of Chicago city center, just off Central Rd.*

Surrounded by a pleasant park and located in a historic 1882 building that in past lives functioned as a general store and post office, CAPANNARI ICE CREAM brings a little bit of Mayberry to this otherwise busy part of Mt. Prospect. Owners Ken and Katie Dix and Jim and Meg Capannari have created a shop that promotes a family atmosphere like no other — which makes sense considering Katie and Meg are sisters. The wholesome activities include tours, Easter egg hunts, a rock, paper, scissor tournament, and screenings of Disney movies under the stars at dusk. On summer nights, parents converse on the wrap-around porch and kids run amok in the grassy park, all while enjoying the best ice cream in the area. The shop produces all the ice cream on the premises and prides itself on using only the finest ingredients it can buy, resulting in ice cream that would make even Aunt Bea smile. Among the flavors that are always available, the **black raspberry chip** is tough to beat. As for the rotating flavors, I recommend either the scrumptious **Maui road**, containing white chocolate, marshmallows, and macadamia nuts, or, if you happen to be in town on St. Patrick's day, the festive **Irish Cream** and **Irish Coffee**.

Carm's Beef & Italian Ice / Mario's Italian Lemonade

ADDRESS 1057 W. Polk St. // 1068 W. Taylor St.
PHONE/WEB 312-738-1046 / www.carms.com // no phone
HOURS Mon–Sat 9a–6p, open Sun during summer, only serves ices May–September // 11a–12a daily, open May–mid-September
DIRECTIONS *Both shops are in the heart of Chicago's Little Italy, near the University of Illinois at Chicago campus.*

There is no disputing that CARM'S BEEF & ITALIAN ICE and MARIO'S ITALIAN LEMONADE are Chicago landmarks; all you need for proof is to visit the Italian ice nexus in the heart of Chicago's Little Italy where, depending on which shop you are visiting, you will find yourself standing on either Fontano Way or Mario DiPaolo's Italian Lemonade Street. These institutions were built by an earlier generation of Fontanos and DiPaolos, and both remain family businesses to this day. As Starbucks and students moved in and Italians moved out, these two shops held their ground and maintained an Italian foothold that now seems to be spawning a renaissance of Old World pride. The founders of the new National Italian American Sports Hall of Fame and the planners behind the Plaza DiMaggio may not admit it, but if not for CARM'S and MARIO'S there may have been no Little Italy to move back to. The reason for their continued success is simple: fresh Italian ices. Both shops offer a selection of ices, including **watermelon**, **cantaloupe**, and **banana**, but the main attraction has always been the **lemon/lemonade**. Visit on a hot summer day and wait in line for a chance to taste these perfect mixtures of tart lemon, sweet sugar, and refreshing shaved ice.

Homer's Ice Cream

ADDRESS 1237 Green Bay Rd., Wilmette
PHONE/WEB 847-251-0477 / www.homersicecream.com
HOURS 11a–10p daily
DIRECTIONS *Thirty minutes north of Chicago city center, on the main road of this affluent suburb.*

Where does one start when describing an ice cream parlor of this caliber? Do you cite the national gold medals it has won or the praise it has received from publications such as *Bon Appetit* and *Chicago* magazine? Should you mention the legendary visits from Al Capone during the shop's early years or the current perfection of the ubiquitous Chicago staple, their Italian beef sub? Maybe, but I think any talk of HOMER'S must first begin with a peach. HOMER'S **peach** has been rated the finest ice cream in the country by the American Culinary Institute, and with one lick I am sure you will agree. Each batch of this marvel contains ripe peaches from Georgia or Michigan, the finest almond extract, and a bit of Georgia nectarines, all combining to create a perfect balance with the shop's creamy, 14 percent butterfat base. Do not expect to find this trademark flavor in January; HOMER'S only serves peach when the fruit is in season, a rule all shops should be forced to follow. If you do visit when peach is not available, try the **prairie berry**, a mixture of blackberries, blueberries, strawberries, and red raspberries, or the **burgundy cherry**, with dark Bordeaux cherries imported directly from France. Also, make sure to ask for a hand-packed pint if you want some ice cream to go, it costs a little more than the machine-packed version, but is far more condensed and well worth the investment. For those who do not want to venture to Wilmette, SWEETIES ICE CREAM PARLOR stocks many flavors from HOMER'S and has the added bonus of being just two blocks north of Wrigley Field.

Mitchell's Candies & Ice Cream

ADDRESS 18211 Dixie Hwy., Homewood
PHONE/WEB 708-799-3835
HOURS Sun–Thu 10a–9:30p, Fri, Sat 10a–10p
DIRECTIONS *Thirty minutes south of Chicago city center.*

MITCHELL'S CANDIES & ICE CREAM has been around since 1931, first on 71st St. on Chicago's South Side and for the last thirty-plus years at its present location on this pleasant suburban shopping street. The shop does not like to rush into any fads and is devoid of glitz, so do not expect to find mix-in ingredients, fro-yo, or fancy neon displays. No, MITCHELL'S prefers to stick to the basics, which in their case entails homemade chocolates and premium ice cream. Thank goodness for this, because although their selection of flavors may be small, their time-tested approach ensures that each batch is of the highest quality. This is one of those shops where it is best to get your flavors in a dish and eat at a table, if for no other reason than to lather on some homemade hot fudge from a personal pitcher — my vote for the best fifty-cent purchase one can make. Like other dual candy and ice cream shops, the best flavor choices are those that combine the two, such as the **chocolate chip** and **mint chocolate chip**, both containing generous chunks and shavings of just-made chocolate. The shop also prepares some great candy, and anyone who visits should definitely try the chocolate-covered Oreos. Oh, and for parents looking to do some one-stop shopping, there is a dentist's office conveniently located next door.

Oberweis Dairy (www.icecreamsource.com)

ADDRESS 101 S. Northwest Hwy.
PHONE/WEB 847-692-9840 / www.oberweisdairy.com
HOURS 9a–10p daily
DIRECTIONS *Over thirty locations throughout Illinois and Missouri.*

The urban legend concerning Mrs. O'Leary's cow in the Great Chicago Fire of 1871 had for years sullied the image of the bovine community in the minds of Chicagoans. The city's slaughter houses have done their part in extracting revenge, but it took Oberweis Dairy to complete the healing process. The company dates back to 1915, when Peter Oberweis started selling excess milk to his neighbors. In the late 1920s he had purchased a part of an existing dairy farm and was delivering milk throughout the area, but it was not until the 1950s that the shop began offering ice cream. Over the next half-century Oberweis became the region's premier ice cream purveyor, and today if you ask residents to name the most famous cow in Chicago, you will likely hear about those that grace the ubiquitous Oberweis Dairy shops rather than the fabled fire starter. To make the product stand out, the company mandates that each batch maintains at least a whopping 18 percent butterfat content. This policy results in a cream lover's paradise of choices among the shop's continually rotating selection of twenty-four flavors, of which I suggest the batter-packed **cookie dough** and the glorious **apple strudel**. If you have the time, sit down with a friend and play a game of chess at one of the available tables set aside for that purpose — alternating moves with samplings of new flavors.

Original Rainbow Cone

ADDRESS 9233 S. Western Ave.
PHONE/WEB 773-238-7075 / www.thebestofchicago.com (not a company site, for mail order purposes only)
HOURS Sun, Fri, Sat 1p–9p, Mon–Thu 3p–9p, closed December–mid-March
DIRECTIONS *South of the city center, just north of the intersection of Western and 95th St. and across from the Evergreen golf course.*

The story behind the ORIGINAL RAINBOW CONE begins where many good ideas start: a childhood dream. As an orphan growing up in Chicago's South Side, Joe Sapp always hungered for more ice cream than he received with his one-cent purchase. In 1926, he realized that dream with the creation of the **original rainbow cone**, a five-flavor concoction that can satisfy even a ten-year-old's sweet tooth. This unique treat is packed with chocolate, strawberry, pistachio, orange sherbet, and **palmer house**, a cherry-flavored ice cream base packed with chunks of cherries and bits of walnut. Today the shop, still at its original location, stands alone on a barren stretch of this Chicago artery, appearing more like a giant pink fortress than the ice cream destination that it is. Lines of customers, rather than marauding hordes, attack these doors, drawn in by the neon cone perched high on the roof, the music coming from the pink piano, and the chance to eat their fill at one of the city's culinary landmarks.

Petersen Ice Cream Company

ADDRESS 1100 Chicago Ave., Oak Park
PHONE/WEB 708-386-6131 / www.petersenicecream.com
HOURS Sun–Thu 8a–9p, Fri, Sat 8a–11p
DIRECTIONS *Ten miles (twenty minutes) due west of downtown Chicago.*

I would like to add to the list of life's golden rules: eat any and all sweets made by the Danes. Hans Petersen, a Danish immigrant, arrived in Oak Park back in 1919, determined to use his Old World training as a confectioner to bring premium ice cream to town. With recipes that used only the freshest ingredients and mandated an 18 percent butterfat content, he opened up PETERSEN ICE CREAM COMPANY and by 1931 was successful enough to move to the current prime location in the town's Frank Lloyd Wright historic district. There have been two groups of owners since his passing in 1963, and both have strictly adhered to the original standards and recipes. This dedication has led to many blue ribbon awards at the Illinois State Fair and a cult-like following that fills the shop throughout the day and well into the night. There are two sections to the shop, a sit-down area that serves diner-type food, and the Sweet Shoppe, a traditional ice cream counter. Although you can get any of the ice cream while sitting, I recommend walking into the Sweet Shoppe to survey the flavors and take advantage of their liberal tasting policy. If you have a tough time deciding, I suggest going with the **New York cherry**, or the devilishly good **cinnamon caramel apple**.

CHALLENGE:

*Your ship definitely has come in if you can handle the **schooner**, five dips of ice cream covered with sliced bananas, urgundy cherries, pineapple and strawberry toppings, and roasted pecans.*

The Plush Horse

ADDRESS 12301 S. 86th Ave., Palos Park
PHONE/WEB 708-448-0550 / www.theplushhorse.com
HOURS Sun 11a–9p, Mon–Thu 6:30a–9p, Fri 6:30a–10:30p, Sat 8a–9p
DIRECTIONS *At the intersection of 123rd St. (McCarthy Rd.) and 86th Ave., thirty minutes southwest of downtown Chicago.*

Set on the corner of a slow intersection and surrounded by woods and fields, THE PLUSH HORSE does its best to bring a bit of small-town Americana to the sprawling Chicago suburbs. From a distance, the shop has the look of an old post house, and it comes as no surprise that it functioned as such at one point during its 110+ years of existence. Other incarnations include time spent as a general store, newlywed's house, and meat market. The pink interior is modern enough to resemble a coffee house, but cozy enough to accommodate a giant stuffed white horse that stands over five feet tall and a carousel horse, complete with pole. One can order coffee, baked goods, and sandwiches, but the real draw is the homemade ice cream, a tradition that started in 1937. The shop gives special attention to their cones, following the mantra "think inside the cone." This results in chocolate-coated and rainbow-sprinkled variations and delicious **homemade drumsticks**. To fill these creations I suggest the **Hawaiian delight**, an expert combination of coconut and pineapple, or the ultra-rich **butter cream**.

MOLINE

Lagomarcino's

ADDRESS 1422 Fifth Ave.
PHONE/WEB 309-764-1814 / www.lagomarcinos.com
HOURS Mon–Sat 9a–5p, closed Sun
DIRECTIONS *In the heart of downtown Moline.*
Also a shop at 2132 E. 11th St. in Davenport.

Twenty-five dollars does not sound like a lot of money these days, but back in 1912 it had the same buying power as roughly $470 today. It's a sum of money that one would have expected Angelo Lagomarcino, who only four years earlier had started up a confectionary in downtown Moline, to have protected like gold. Angelo, however, had foresight, and despite his wife's protestations, agreed to pay a traveling salesman twenty-five dollars for a secret **hot fudge** recipe. His instincts were right, as this secret blend continues to attract fudge-o-holics to this day, each waiting to lather on this glorious goo according to their liking atop a sundae. This purchase is emblematic of the investment and care that each of the four generations of Lagomarcinos who have managed the shop have taken over the past century to maintain this quintessential American soda parlor. Original Tiffany-style lamps, mahogany booths, terrazzo floors, and a metal ceiling all create an Old World ambiance that make one want to indulge in a gorging of sweets. While the aforementioned sundae is a must, make sure to also try the homemade and scrumptious **black raspberry** and **English toffee** ice creams. Whatever you choose, this is one investment you will not regret.

COLUMBUS

Zaharako's

ADDRESS 329 Washington St.
PHONE/WEB 812-379-9329
HOURS Sun 12p–4p, Mon–Thu 10a–4p, Fri, Sat 10a–5p
DIRECTIONS *Fifty miles south of Indianapolis. The shop is in the heart of town, between Third and Fourth streets.*

New York. Boston. San Francisco. Columbus, Indiana? All were among the cities ranked at the top of an American Institute of Architects' list recognizing architectural innovation and design. This is quite an honor for a town with less than 40,000 inhabitants, but as anyone who has visited Columbus knows, this is no ordinary town. Since the construction of the landmark First Christian Church in 1942, the community's companies, congregations, and residents have financed building upon building designed by the world's top modern architects, earning the city the nickname Athens of the Prairie. This moniker is especially fitting because ZAHARAKO'S, Columbus's original landmark, was first called The Greek. Today the shop is run by third generation Zaharakos and continues to be a destination worthy of this special town. The modern movement has not made the slightest inroads here; rather ZAHARAKO'S appearance seems to have hardly changed during the past century. Among the shop's unique fixtures are the quartered oak panels that have adorned the walls since the shop's opening in 1900, a German organ complete with 185 pipes and dating back to 1908, and two twin marble and Mexican onyx soda fountains that were originally displayed at the 1904 St. Louis World's Fair. The shop stopped making its own ice cream a while ago, but the ice cream parlor ambiance is too perfect to ignore. I recommend visiting the shop for lunch, ordering the peculiar cheese br-gr, a grilled cheese mixed with meat sauce, and washing it down with a banana split topped with **homemade hot fudge.**

Ritter's Frozen Custard

ADDRESS 3219 W. County Line Rd., Greenwood
PHONE/WEB 317-594-9444 / www.ritters.com
HOURS Sun–Thu 11a–10p, Fri, Sat 11a–11p
DIRECTIONS *Over 50 locations throughout Indiana, Ohio, South Carolina, Michigan, Florida, Tennessee, and Texas.*

The story behind RITTER'S is a testament to the allure of fresh ice cream. John Ritter, founder of the present-day franchise, first got hooked on ice cream while he was a teenager working after school at an ice cream parlor. During idle moments he would eat just-made ice cream, before it had been packed and frozen, thus creating a permanent craving for this ultra-smooth delicacy. Over the next forty years John joined the Navy, married, raised six children, and opened up an animation production studio, all the while hungering for fresh ice cream. In the late 1980s, John decided to open up his own shop and, together with his wife, Bonny, toured the country in search of the freshest ice cream available. After many samples, they concluded that frozen custard replicated the just-from-the-machine taste most accurately. Following several months spent creating their recipe, the couple opened the first RITTER'S in Franklin, Indiana in 1989. The shop was an instant success and over the past fifteen years RITTER'S has grown into a fifty-shop, seven-state franchise. This growth threatens to make RITTER'S too large for the pages of this book, but their commitment to producing high-quality custard in each shop on a daily basis and their no frills, what-you-see-is-what-you-get philosophy continues to make every shop feel like a mom-and-pop enterprise. **Vanilla** and **chocolate** are always available as well as daily specials ranging from **red raspberry** to **rocky road**. John has finally satisfied his craving and has been kind enough to let the rest of us share in his indulgence.

MADISON

Mundt's Candies (JWI Confectionery)

ADDRESS 207 W. Main St.
PHONE/WEB 812-265-6171 / www.mundtscandies.com
HOURS Open Sat and four weekdays on average; please call to confirm before visiting
DIRECTIONS *In the heart of the downtown historic district.*

Set in a quaint river town, MUNDT'S CANDIES is housed in a historic three-story brick building that dates back to 1835. Over time, various businesses sold boots, hats, and telegrams from this locale, but it was not until Walter Mundt moved his candy shop to these premises in 1917 that the building became Madison's must-visit destination. Fish candies were what put the shop and for that matter the town on the map. A Madison holiday tradition, these colorful little treats date back to the mid-nineteenth century and were once so

popular that three separate candy makers were needed to keep up with the demand. MUNDT'S distinguished itself by also serving homemade ice cream in a classic parlor setting. In 1966, the Mundts retired and the shop stood idle for thirty years until Maryanne Imes and her mother, Berneta Wolf, purchased the building in 1996. Their one-year renovation plan turned into a two-year, full-scale restoration project that included an elevator rehabilitation, a demolition and subsequent rebuilding of a two-story addition, and the refurbishing of all of the candy, soda fountain, and ice cream equipment. Maryanne was so concerned with getting everything just right that she even gave the shop a new name, JWI CONFECTIONERY, just in case her offerings did not match the high expectations people had for the MUNDT'S brand. This precaution was not necessary, for Maryanne, her husband, Tom, and her continually supportive mother have successfully recreated this Madison landmark, a shop that again proudly carries on the MUNDT'S tradition. While the fish candy, which is still created in the same third-floor kitchen, is a must, the homemade ice cream, produced using a machine that dates back to 1948, is also memorable. Apron-clad servers and wood booths make this a place to linger while you tackle a sundae or a double dip of **red raspberry chocolate chip**.

CHALLENGE:

*The description for the **'37 flood** sundae is correct when it claims inundate, rather than serve, to six people. It is comprised ten scoops, seven toppings, nana, whipped cream, nuts, erries, and chocolate fish — a combination I guarantee will add to your buoyancy.*

Section 4

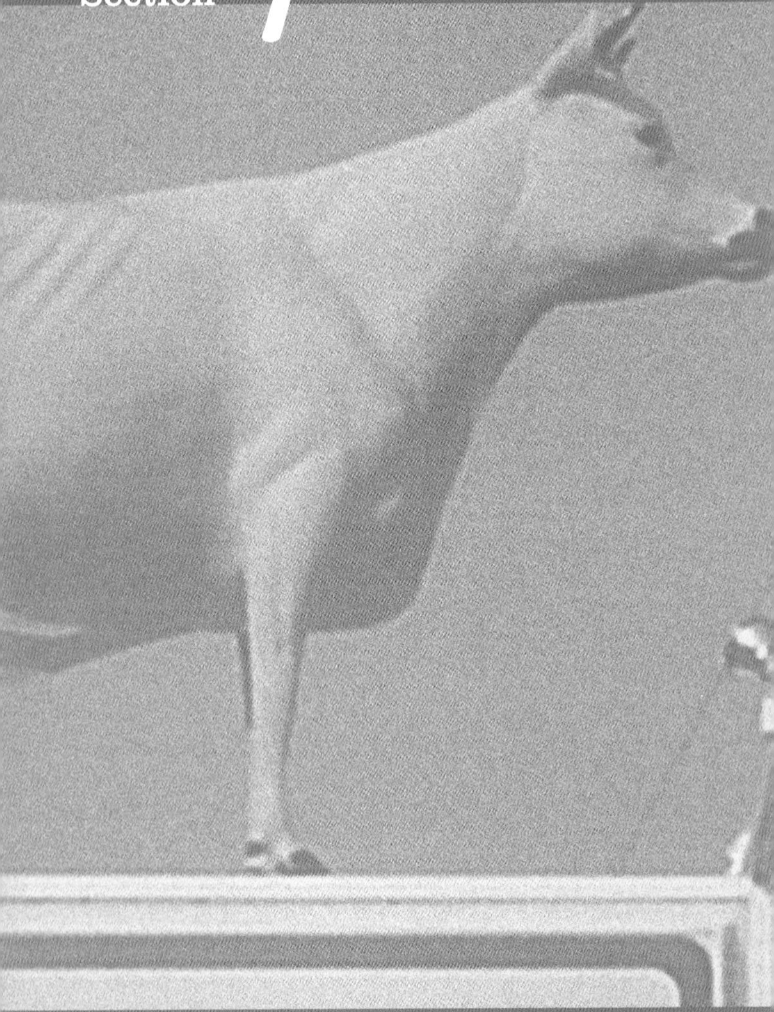

MICHIGAN OHIO

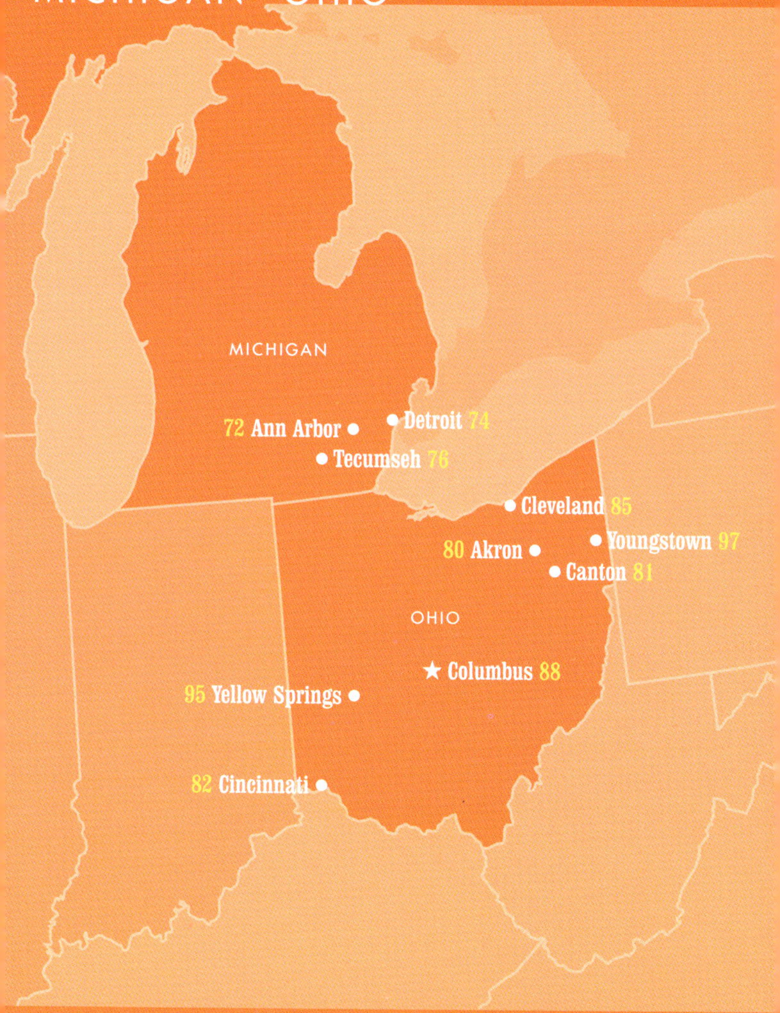

ANN ARBOR

Stuchhi's

ADDRESS 302 S. State St.
PHONE/WEB 734-662-1700
HOURS Sun 12p–10:30p, Mon–Sat 11a–10:30p
DIRECTIONS *Seven locations in Michigan and fourteen in Texas. State Street shop is on Ann Arbor's main drag, between E. Liberty St. and E. William St.*

The first STUCCHI'S was started in 1986 and two other shops followed in the ensuing three years, giving the company the strongest ice cream presence in this quintessential college town. In 2000, however, two major changes occurred: new owners took over the State Street location, traditionally the company's busiest and most profitable, and Ben & Jerry's opened up next door. Customers braced for the worst, fearing that the shop would lose its charm under new management and not be able to compete against the ice cream giant. Conversely, the new owners maintained all that was great about the business and even set about expanding through licensing agreements. Within a four-year span four new locations have opened up in Michigan, and thanks in part to ice cream lover and STUCCHI'S-franchise owner Rudy Tomjanovich (ex-NBA coach and Michigan alum), fourteen STUCCHI'S have been established in Texas. There are several reasons for this success, including a spacious, chic setting, and an array of tasty ice cream, including the **Johnny cashew**, a mixture of vanilla yogurt, caramel, and chocolate-covered cashews. The real draw however, are the extra-thick **smushins**, combinations of fresh ice cream or frozen yogurt mixed with a choice of toppings. Customers are invited to create their own unique smushins or order one of the time-tested favorites off the board. If you choose the latter route I recommend **vanilla with strawberries and fresh bananas** or the heavenly **French silk with Heath bar**.

DETROIT VICINITY

Ray's Ice Cream

ADDRESS 4233 Coolidge Hwy., Royal Oak
PHONE/WEB 888-549-5256 / www.raysicecream.com
HOURS Sun 12p–10p, Mon–Sat 10a–10p
DIRECTIONS *Fifteen minutes northwest of downtown Detroit, between 13- and 14-mile roads.*

Who knew that molds could taste so good? Ray Stevens and his wife Bernice founded RAY'S ICE CREAM in 1958 and today a third generation of Stevenses keeps watch over this local treasure. The classic waist-high counter with low stools and ice cream specialties such as **fat Elvis**, a mixture of bananas and peanut butter, and the pineapple-flavored **blue moon**, make the shop a worthy entry in their own right, but molds are what make this shop truly special. Since its opening, RAY'S has specialized in the nearly forgotten art of molding ice cream into life-like objects. This shop's mastery of this practice has made RAY'S the favored provider of molds to restaurants, clubs, and individuals across the country. Over eighty types of molds are available for special order, with varieties including cooing doves, pigs, sailboats, and Santa Claus. While most of the molds are solid ice cream delicately flavored with natural ingredients, RAY'S also makes some cordials that have at their core different dessert liqueurs. So visit RAY'S, eat some tasty ice cream, check out their molds, and decide which liqueur-loaded ice cream pig you want to order for your next party.

Stroh's

ADDRESS 31359 Harper Ave., St. Clair Shores
PHONE/WEB 586-294-2440
HOURS Sun 1p–9p, Mon–Sat 12p–10p
DIRECTIONS *Twenty minutes north of Detroit, near the shores of Lake St. Clair.*

STROH'S is spoken here. I'm no teetotaler, but I think prohibition was the best thing that ever happened to Detroit, because without it STROH'S ice cream would have never existed. In 1919 James W. Stroh was seeking ways of keeping his brewery afloat as the country began to ban the sale of its much-loved beer. A chocolate ice cream fanatic, Stroh realized that the brewery's refrigeration facilities could be used to store mass quantities of his favorite treat and thus ordered that it become the new indulgence the company would provide for the people of Michigan. Stroh took special care to taste all of the ice cream flavors before they were first distributed, and thanks to his superior palate, by the time prohibition was rolled back the ice-cream business had blossomed and the company found itself in better position than before the ban. Today STROH'S is the best selling ice cream brand in Detroit. The listed retail shop is basic, but eighty-five years of experience is evident in each tasting — even the late James Stroh would approve of the decadent **triple chocolate overload**.

TECUMSEH

The Chocolate Vault

ADDRESS 110-116 W. Chicago Blvd.
PHONE/WEB 517-423-7602 / www.chocolatevault.com
HOURS Sun 12p–7p, Mon–Thu 9:30a–7p, Fri, Sat 9:30a–10p
DIRECTIONS *Twenty-five miles southwest of Ann Arbor in the center of town.*

Set on the main drag of this quaint hamlet, THE CHOCOLATE VAULT is both a historical and gastronomical destination. The building that houses the shop has been a downtown Tecumseh fixture since 1849 and, thanks in part to a restoration in 1986 by the current owners, is listed as part of the Tecumseh Downtown Historic District on the National Register of Historic Places. To reach the ice cream parlor one must walk through the chocolate and candy shop, which over the years has functioned as a public library, diner, barber shop, and harness outfitter. A plethora of enticing candies and a waft of chocolate fill the room, making it difficult for choc-o-holics and those with a sweet-tooth to pass through. The strong-willed that make it to the parlor unscathed will be thankful, because the chocolates are just as good when you get them to go and, trust me, you will want an empty stomach. The parlor is true to its historic banking roots, with patrons ordering from the marble counter that once separated customers from tellers, and the namesake vault on display. Customers are encouraged to walk around and check out the old photographs and postcards that provide a visual history of the town and building over more than a century's time. When you've satisfied your curiosity, walk to the counter and order a **security split** or **the treasurer's transaction**, the shop's respective versions of a banana split and hot fudge sundae, both with the added addition of homemade buttered pecans.

CHALLENGE:

The great chocolate vault caper *contains four scoops, four toppings, whipped cream, buttered pecans, and a cherry. After one of these, all plans of a heist and speedy getaway will be forgotten.*

EXTRA SCOOPS

Sundae Best

Like the story behind the introduction of the first cone, the origin of the ice cream sundae is contested. Over a half dozen cities lay claim to its genesis, but the following three tales are the most credible.

Version 1: Back in 1881 in the small town of Two Rivers, Wisconsin, a customer named George Hallauer asked Edward Berner, owner of the local ice cream parlor, for a dish of ice cream topped with chocolate syrup for the grand total of a nickel. After a little resistance, Berner obliged and tried it for himself. One tasting convinced him that this new delicacy was worthy of a place on his menu, but only on Sundays because the cost of the ice cream and syrup was higher than the five-cent price. One day a young girl walked in and ordered a dish of ice cream "with that stuff on top," and was told that it was only available on Sundays. To this she replied that they could "pretend it was Sunday," and not having the heart to deny a little girl twice, Berner served her the sundae and thereafter made it available every day of the week.

Version 2: During the 1880s, Evanston, Illinois, was a right pious town. The Sabbath was strictly reserved for devotion and rest, and any work or extracurricular activities were frowned upon. Visits to ice cream parlors were singled out as being too frivolous for such a holy day, and town elders went so far as to ban the sale of ice cream sodas on Sundays.

William Garwood, owner of Garwood's drugstore, circumvented this rule by serving ice cream topped with syrup — sans soda — thus creating the Sunday. Outsmarted, the devout demanded that the name be changed, and thus the "sundae" was born.

Version 3: Religion also plays a part in Ithaca, New York's, claim of origin. Their story maintains that in 1891, the Reverend John Scott stopped by the C.C. Platt drugstore after delivering his Sunday sermon. In a moment of divine inspiration, the minister requested a dish of ice cream topped with cherry soda syrup. The combination was a success and together the drugstore's owner and Scott decided to dub the new creation in honor of its day of creation.

Whether any or all of these stories are accurate, the important point is that the sundae caught on and eventually became a nationwide favorite. Americans love excess, and the sundae elevated ice cream to a new level by allowing customers to further specialize their orders with the addition of sauces, fruits, and decadent toppings. From the classic banana split to the ever-popular turtle, sundaes are a true American creation and the ultimate indulgence.

AKRON

Strickland's Frozen Custard

ADDRESS 1809 Triplett Blvd.
PHONE/WEB 330-733-0133 / www.stricklands.info
HOURS Summer: 11a–11p daily, closed December–March
DIRECTIONS *In the southern part of the city, across from the Akron Fulton International Airport. Over a dozen other locations in Ohio, Colorado, California, and Florida.*

When times are tough, eat frozen custard. In the mid-1930s in the midst of the Great Depression, Bill Strickland, who had perfected a **vanilla** frozen custard recipe while working at a nearby dairy plant, was looking for a place to set up shop. He knew that despite hard times people still craved entertainment and thus decided to open up right across from the town's airport — planes were still a relatively new and exciting invention and, more important, did not cost a cent to watch. Throughout the week and especially on weekends, customers would gather to enjoy Bill's affordable indulgence as they gazed at the planes soaring skyward or landing a few hundred yards away. Thanks to this convergence of spectacle and vanilla nirvana, STRICKLAND'S thrived under the watch of Bill and subsequent owner Larry Margroff. Today STRICKLAND'S FROZEN CUSTARD is run by Larry's children, who over the last few years have undertaken an ambitious franchising program — with eleven locations open in Ohio, two in Colorado, and one each in California and Florida. While these newer locales, each of which utilizes hand-crafted ice cream batch freezers built to replicate the production of the seventy-year-old hand-built machines of the Triplett Boulevard locale, produce the same rich custard, the Akron shop remains the best place to enjoy your cone and watch the planes come in. Bill Strickland's vanilla custard is still served, and **chocolate** has become a permanent menu fixture along with a rotating flavor of the day, of which I had the pleasure of devouring the **black raspberry** and the **piña colada**.

CANTON

Taggarts Ice Cream Parlor

ADDRESS 1401 Fulton Rd. NW
PHONE/WEB 330-452-6844
HOURS Mon–Thu 11a–11p, Fri–Sun 11a–12a
DIRECTIONS *Northwest of the city center.*

Mean Joe Green. Sweetness. Bronco Nagurski. The Bittner. All are names forever associated with Canton, Ohio, but while the first three are nicknames of football greats that are enshrined in the nearby hall of fame, the fourth is a specialty at Taggarts, Canton's ice cream parlor of choice. Long before football became America's obsession, Taggarts had made this industrial town a destination. The shop opened in 1926 and is one of the longest running downtown businesses. Over the years, the shop has been through several ownership changes, but its commitment to serving high grade ice cream has never wavered. I do not know where they get them, but Taggarts seems to have the best pecans on earth, making their **butter pecan** and **chocolate pecan** among the best versions of either flavor I have ever tasted. For those looking to make a pit stop, Taggarts has some good diner fare in addition to its ice cream offerings.

CHALLENGE:

*The aforementioned **bittner**, composed of five scoops of vanilla ice cream — roughly three quarters of a pound! — blended with a healthy dose of homemade chocolate sauce and topped off with a scoop of pecans, is so good that it would make even Mean Joe Green smile.*

CINCINNATI & VICINITY

Aglamesis Brothers

ADDRESS 3046 Madison Rd., Oakley Square
PHONE/WEB 513-531-5196 / www.aglamesis.com
HOURS Summer: Sun 12p–10p, Mon–Thu 10a–10p, Fri, Sat 10a–11p; shorter hours in winter
DIRECTIONS *Fifteen minutes northeast of downtown Cincinnati; another shop is located in Montgomery Square, 9899 Montgomery Rd.*

How classic is AGLAMESIS? Three words: horse team delivery. Back in 1908, Thomas and Nicholas Aglamesis, recent immigrants from Sparta, Greece, opened their first ice cream parlor, The Metropolitan, on the east side of town. Since refrigeration units were not an option, the brothers' hand-churned ice cream was frozen using rock salt and then delivered to wealthy residents by way of their speedy horse team. By 1913 the business was profitable enough to open up the Oakley Square location, which still exists today. The shop is now being run by a combination of second and third generations of Aglamesises, and the Portuguese marble bar, Tiffany-style lamps, tile floors, and resplendent pink ambiance continue to make a lasting impression on modern-day customers. In addition to ice cream, the shop has long produced homemade chocolates and candies, but I suggest filling up on the ice cream and ordering your opera creams, pecan clusters, and buckeyes to go. The ice cream is still produced in small batches to insure a low overrun and high butterfat content, and the end results are unbeatable flavors including the seasonal **rum bisque**, with juicy plump raisins, and the **Dutch Holland chocolate**, a flavor so nice they named it twice.

Graeter's

ADDRESS 2145 Reading Rd.
PHONE/WEB 513-721-3323, 800-721-3323 / www.graeters.com
HOURS 7a–10:45p, listed shop is closed on Sun, but others are open seven days a week
DIRECTIONS *Twelve company-owned shops in and around Cincinnati and twenty-three franchised shops throughout Ohio and Northern Kentucky.*

GRAETER'S transcends the limits of ice cream. Each year GRAETER'S is ranked as one of the top ten ice cream parlors in the country by several media sources, and, even more notably, has been proclaimed the best tasting ice cream in the world by my father, an ice cream fanatic. The first I heard of the company was when I was in college. During one of my weekly calls home, my father would not stop praising the quality of the six pints of GRAETER'S he had just been sent as a gift. I got off the phone eager to try this ice cream that had my Dad swooning, but to my surprise when I returned home for a weekend visit three days later, he had finished off the entire shipment. For the next decade a sampling remained elusive, haunting me whenever I met an Ohioan who would invariably mention that I had not really tasted ice cream until I had been to GRAETER'S. Eventually I made a trip to Cincinnati with the sole purpose of tasting their flavors, and boy oh boy was it worth it. Like a Rembrandt portrait, a Mozart concerto, or the Icky Shuffle, the shop's French pot method of making ice cream proves that some things cannot be improved upon. The process has remained the same for more than a century, producing two-gallon batches of their scrumptious ice cream at a time. The method calls for rotating chilled, bucket-like pots as the mixture is swirled

CONTINUED >

GRAETER'S CONTINUED

along the sides and then scraped off by workers wielding specially designed stainless steel scrapers. This time-consuming process prevents excess air from entering the batters, thus ensuring dense, flavorful results. The shop creates its renowned chip flavors by pouring in liquid chocolate during the mixing process, which produces odd-sized chocolate chips and chunks. Among these flavors, the **black raspberry chip** and the **chocolate mocha chip**, tasting more like coffee than a cup of joe, are my favorites. If you prefer no chips, try the **butter pecan**, which, being true to its name, tastes so rich and creamy that you could spread it on toast.

Honey Hut Homemade Ice Cream Shoppe

ADDRESS 4674 State Rd.
PHONE/WEB 216-749-7077
HOURS 11a–10p daily, closed mid-November–mid-March
DIRECTIONS *Four locations in the greater Cleveland area.*

Frank Page opened the first HONEY HUT in 1974 as a side business to supplement his job as a fireman, and within a few months the shop had become so popular that he made a permanent switch from fire to ice. Over the past thirty years he has gradually expanded the business to the current four locations and today with the help of his five grown children the HUT has become Cleveland's favorite place to cool down. The business is aptly named, because during the summer the shop resembles the inside of a hive, with customers buzzing to and fro as they wait for a chance to order. This frenzy is on account of the HUT's practice of adding plenty of honey to every flavor, resulting in concoctions that can only be described as nectar-licious. In fact, different honey blends are used for different batches, each drawing out its own unique, subtle flavor. This technique results in an outstanding selection that includes the **orange blossom**, a super creamy delight, and the **honey pecan**, a treat worthy of any queen bee.

Malley's Chocolates

ADDRESS 14822 Madison Ave., Lakewood
PHONE/WEB 216-529-6262 / www.malleys.com
HOURS Sun 12p–10p, Mon–Sat 10a–10p
DIRECTIONS *Four locations serving ice cream in the greater Cleveland area; listed shop is ten minutes west of downtown Cleveland.*

MALLEY'S CHOCOLATES has been satisfying Clevelanders' sweet tooths since 1935. The company's main focus has always been chocolate, as evidenced by their 60,000-square-foot chocolate factory that supplies fifteen retail stores and distributes boxes of candy throughout the United States. While their dark chocolate nutmallows and chocolate-covered pretzels may enjoy a national reputation, MALLEY'S four ice cream parlors are special in their own right. For people who have yet to visit the Madison Avenue location, try to visualize an over-the-top candy and ice cream parlor and then paint that fantasy pink and green. You must first walk through a room choc-full-o-chocolate to get to the old-fashioned counter. Here you can take a seat on a high stool and peruse a menu that has all their favorites, including knockout flavors **toffee crunch** and **cherry vanilla**. For those wanting to devour the giant **turtle sundae**, a mountain of chocolate ice cream drowned in a wave of butterscotch, pecans, and fresh whipped cream, I suggest getting a seat in the Alice in Wonderland–themed back room — that way not as many people will see you loosening your belt as you near the last bites. Whatever you order, make sure to take advantage of the decadent homemade hot fudge that customers are allowed to dispense to their own liking.

Mitchell's Homemade

ADDRESS 26161 Detroit Rd., Westlake
PHONE/WEB 440-250-0952
HOURS Sun–Thu 11a–10p, Fri, Sat 11a–11p
DIRECTIONS *Three locations in the greater Cleveland area, this shop is fifteen minutes west of downtown Cleveland.*

MITCHELL'S HOMEMADE is like the mysterious new kid at a school who within weeks has become the starting quarterback, is dating the prettiest girl, and is beloved by classmates and teachers alike. The business, which was founded by brothers Mike and Pete Mitchell in 1999, seems almost too perfect, with no detail having been forgotten despite its relatively short history. All of the shops are beautifully furnished, with sleek wood floors and custom-built chairs making it appear more lounge than parlor. Yet, this plush setting remains family-oriented, leaving aside enough space to hang crayon depictions of their logo drawn by their littlest customers. Likewise, the brothers' carefully crafted vision carries over into the creation of everything sold at the shop, from the homemade hot fudge to the waffle cones that are baked fresh several times daily. A special premium is placed on quality ingredients, with a hand-painted manifesto on a wall proudly proclaiming that the ice cream contains vanilla from Madagascar, chocolate from Holland, mouth-watering fruits from the world's best growing regions, and natural extracts from Europe. These ingredients unite to create drool-inducing flavors such as **strawberry** and **key lime pie**. By combining all of these attributes, MITCHELL'S HOMEMADE could be the class president as well.

COLUMBUS & VICINITY

Jeni's Fresh Ice Creams

ADDRESS 59 Spruce St.
PHONE/WEB 614-228-9960 / www.jenisicecreams.com
HOURS Sun 11a–5p, Tue–Fri 9a–7p, Sat 8a–5p
DIRECTIONS *Located in Columbus's North Market, one block north of Nationwide Arena.*

At the age of 22, Jeni Britton opened up Scream Ice Cream in Columbus's historic North Market with the goal of serving patisserie-quality ice cream — every flavor made from scratch with the finest ingredients and without artificial flavorings. Having dabbled in fine art and worked at a French bakery, she was uniquely qualified to achieve this goal, and the shop quickly gained a devoted following of customers craving her unusual flavors. While Jeni was a natural ice cream artisan, her business sense was still developing and some choices, such as not being able to guarantee the availability of any particular flavor on a given day,

prevented the shop from consistently drawing in the vanilla- and chocolate-loving ice cream public. In 2000 she closed Scream down, focusing instead on making ice cream for restaurants and saving up for a new endeavor. Two years later, JENI'S FRESH ICE CREAMS opened for business in the adjacent stall with the same inventive spirit, but with a partner, Jeni's husband Charly Bauer, focused on business matters. Charly's brother and Jeni's sister also now work for the company, and together this family has combined their different strengths to build a successful business in a short time. One of the changes has been to establish a menu of signature flavors that are always available. If you are not in driving distance from JENI'S you may not want to read the following list of flavors, the cravings may just overcome you. **Wild berry lavender, cocoa curry cocoa, strawberry buttermilk**, and **mango with cardamom and whole pistachios** are just a few of the sensational flavors that always await lucky patrons. JENI'S also continues to create new flavors, such as **Ohio sweet corn with blackberry** and the delectable **lemon blueberry**, utilizing the seasonal produce from the surrounding farmers' market stalls. After an initial bump in the road, Jeni and family have created a truly extraordinary shop, bringing gourmet ice cream to Columbus and serving flavors that are as memorable as any in the land.

CHALLENGE:

*Part of the shop's philosophy is to inspire people to try new things, and as a supplement to its unlimited tasting policy, Jeni's offers the six-ounce, ree-scoop **trio ($3)** and the twelve-unce, five-scoop **study ($5)**. Order ne of these and make sure one of the scoops is **salted caramel**, a ncoction of burnt sugar, Fleur de Sel French sea salt), and Plugra butter (the butter of choice for bakers) that can only be described as culinary genius.*

EXTRA SCOOPS

Delicious Obsession

Some customers balked at paying more than four dollars for a small cup of gelato when Philadelphia's CAPOGIRO GELATO ARTISANS opened in late 2002. That was before they tasted what's been lauded as some of the best gelati outside of Italy — a product filled with local fruit picked that morning, mixed with dairy from grass-fed cows that have not been treated with hormones, and lovingly churned in small batches by CAPOGIRO'S owners. CAPOGIRO is one of a small but growing group of ice cream shops whose owners take obsession with quality to a whole new level. Make that a whole old level, since many of the people behind places like **Capogiro**, New York's IL LABORATORIO DEL GELATO, MALLARD ICE CREAM in Bellingham, Washington, THE BENT SPOON in Princeton, New Jersey, JENI'S FRESH ICE CREAMS in Columbus, Ohio, and Minneapolis's CREMA CAFÉ and SONNY'S, say they're returning to an old-fashioned way of making ice cream. Buzz words like organic, sustainable, handcrafted, seasonal, and artisanal are hot right now, but these owners insist that what they're doing is about taste and tradition, not hype. "We don't want to use pastes, colors, and imitation flavors," says Gabrielle Carbone, one half of the husband-and-wife team that opened THE BENT SPOON in 2004. "We want to go back to the old way where you crack the eggs and cut up the fruit. We try to use organic whenever we can and if we can support a local farm or orchard, we do."

Carbone and her quality-obsessed compatriots take their processes seriously, grinding spices by hand, roasting nuts, grating ginger, pureeing fresh fruit, chopping chocolate, infusing cream with spices or fresh-roasted coffee, making mix-ins such as nougat by hand, insisting on small batches, and in general employing methods used by world-class chefs. It's a process that Carrie Gustafson, co-owner of SONNY'S and CREMA CAFÉ, likens to making fine wine. "We work with our ingredients to create balance, depth, and layers of flavor." Ben Scholtz, who bought MALLARD ICE CREAM in 2001, wants to take advantage of the fact that he only makes one product. "When I'm at work, I'm only focusing on one thing: making the best ice cream possible." Similarly, **Jeni Britton**, who opened JENI'S FRESH ICE CREAMS in 2002, views the creation of ice cream as an art project — something that should be approached with a keen sense of quality and style. "Like a shoemaker or a tailor, I sculpt ice creams from ingredients that I care about, that I have a connection to," says Britton. "Beautiful ingredients, traditional methods, and a spotless kitchen should be valued above all."

These ice cream makers tend to have personal relationships with the farmers who supply them. "I'm less concerned about the fact that it is certified organic than I am that it is from cows who are treated well and that it is from a local supplier who I can talk to," Britton says. Stephanie Reitano, who started CAPOGIRO with her husband, John, prefers to purchase fruit locally so it can be picked at the peak of ripeness when it has the highest sugar content, unlike fruits that are picked early so they can be shipped across the globe. She raves about local produce, like beautiful "teeny-tiny" grape-size strawberries and "hideous looking" but incredibly sweet apples. "We strictly adhere to seasonality, but not to be trendy," says Reitano. "I have found that it is far better tasting, period." THE BENT SPOON'S Carbone agrees, gushing, "We were lucky to get truly awesome organic verbena all summer long from a local farmer." Carbone takes much of her inspiration from what's available at the farmers' market. "When we opened, it was so easy to come up with flavors because there was this wealth of organic produce," she says.

Of course, not every ingredient is available locally, so these ice cream makers search all over the world for the very best ingredients, such as Reitano's champagne mangoes, chosen for their superior taste and creamy texture, Scholtz's Bernard Callebaut chocolate and Nielsen-Massey vanilla, and Britton's Asian lychees and French wild blueberries. Britton sources her pomegranate molasses and rose water from a Middle Eastern market near her shop and gets candied fennel seeds and cardamom pods from an Indian market. In addition to the many herbs, peppers, and fruits that IL LABORATORIO DEL GELATO's owner, Jon Snyder, gets from local farmers' markets, he sources black sesame paste and seeds from Japan, and hazelnut, pistachio, and coffee paste from Italy. "We find the best possible source and go there," says Gustafson of SONNY'S and CREMA CAFÉ, who has hundreds of suppliers. "It sometimes becomes a logistical nightmare, but it's so worth it."

While flavorings are important, great ice cream starts with a great base. As Scholtz says, "The cleaner the base, the more you can taste the flavors, and even strong flavors are improved by a clean base." At THE BENT SPOON, Carbone and her husband, Matt Errico, mix the base daily from fresh ingredients. At SONNY'S and CREMA CAFÉ, Gustafson and co-owner

Ron Siron use all organic cream, milk, and sugar. Meanwhile, at Capogiro, Reitano uses dairy from a single herd of pasture-fed cows. The farmer has to tell Reitano when the onion grass is out so she can smell the milk before using it to make sure it hasn't picked up an oniony taste.

While the overarching themes in all of these ice creams and gelati are great flavor and texture, there are definite elements of social and environmental responsibility at play here too. Talking about the international movement to preserve food traditions, Britton says, "Slow Food is casually making its way toward ice cream." Likewise, Gustafson says she's noticed that "people are becoming more interested and educated about what they put in their mouths." Reitano jokes that "being responsible and supporting farmers and not eating McDonald's is completely selfish," noting that it all comes down to great-tasting food. "Being very conscious about what you eat can be cool," she says, "It doesn't have to be granola."

Ironically, growing consumer interest in high-quality food presents a distinct challenge for these purveyors, who are constantly being approached by people who want them to expand and franchise. "What we do can't be mass-produced," says Scholtz of **Mallard**. Snyder, who sold his first gelato shop, Ciao Bella, and watched it later grow into a national player along the lines of Ben & Jerry's, is wary of rapid expansion. "We're growing continuously and my number one concern by far is that I do not want to compromise the quality," he says, adding that the "Starbucks, McDonalds, etc. phenomenon" saddens him. "I am not interested in seeing hundreds of 'labs' around the world," he says. "I think it is so much more interesting when someone puts their own name and stamp on something."

Johnson's Real Ice Cream

ADDRESS 2728 E. Main St., Bexley
PHONE/WEB 614-231-0014 / www.johnsonsrealicecream.com
HOURS Sun 2p–11p, Mon–Sat 10a–11p
DIRECTIONS *Reviewed shop is just east of downtown Columbus, one other location at 7111 E. Main St, Reynoldsburg, OH.*

JOHNSON'S REAL ICE CREAM is a fixture in Bexley, and is considered as much a local hangout as it is an ice cream parlor. Four generations of the Johnson/Wilcoxon clan have worked the counter since the shop's founding in 1950, each maintaining a first-name familiarity with their loyal customers. These customers are typically either children, or adults who have been coming since they were kids; each having spent time watching the production process through the window opening onto the ice cream laboratory. Fudge, a great word and a better topping, seems to have dropped off the radar screen in our diet-obsessed culture, but thankfully there are shops like JOHNSON'S that continue to serve this most decadent of treats. The shop's fudge-related specialties include **fudge splits**, **vanilla fudge pies**, **pecan fudge logs**, and the **French butter fudge** ice cream, which is proudly described as having a higher butterfat content (14 percent) than other flavors. Also available are the award-winning **pure vanilla**, a **fresh strawberry sherbet** that is only offered from May to July, and the famous **buckeye**, a scoop of peanut butter/chocolate chip ice cream dipped in chocolate that is shipped in packs of forty-eight throughout the country via next-day air for game-day delivery.

YELLOW SPRINGS

Young's Jersey Dairy

ADDRESS 6880 Springfield Xenia Rd. (Rt. 68)
PHONE/WEB 937-325-0629 / www.youngsdairy.com
HOURS 6a–10p daily
DIRECTIONS *Twenty miles east of Dayton, five and a half miles south of I-70.*

More county fair than ice cream parlor, YOUNG'S JERSEY DAIRY is an amusement destination that hosts over a million customers each year. This complex offers visitors an array of dining and activity options, including two restaurants, a bakery, a miniature golf course, batting cages, a golf range, and a petting zoo. The business has its own herd of cows, but in order to meet the ice cream demands of its customers, it also purchases milk from a local co-op. This decision to use local suppliers is emblematic of the company's commitment to the surrounding community. Another example of this commitment is the Udder Chaos charity program. Each year hand-decorated cows are spread throughout the complex — hanging from trees, sitting on perches, and grazing in gardens. At the end of the peak season these creations are auctioned off, with proceeds going to local schools, organizations, and charities. While the attractions and hometown support have helped make YOUNG'S a favorite stop for people throughout the region, the ice cream is the real reason for its continued success. Bus loads of people come to eat the flavors of the week, and lucky customers arrive on days when the shop is offering the unbeatable **peaches & cream** or the heavenly **rocky road**.

YOUNGSTOWN

Handel's Homemade Ice Cream & Yogurt

ADDRESS 3931 Handel's Ct.
PHONE/WEB 330-788-0356 / www.handelsicecream.com
HOURS 11a–10p daily
DIRECTIONS *Over 20 locations throughout Ohio, Pennsylvania, and Indiana; this shop is just south of downtown Youngstown.*

How good is HANDEL'S? I once witnessed three people waiting to be served during the middle of a blizzard ... and the shop was not even open. Alice Handel started the business in 1945 by selling her homemade ice cream at her husband's gas station. Her hand-cranked concoctions were a hit, and she soon opened this shop on what was then Vermont Court, a one-way alley. As the years rolled by, the shop's fame and following grew, and the shack became one of the most visited locations in town, at one point serving over 1,700 customers in a three-hour period. So revered was the shop, that in 1985, Alice was awarded a key to the city and the alley was renamed Handel's Court. In that same year, after four decades of dishing out Youngstown's best ice cream, Alice sold the business to Leonard Fisher. Under Leonard's watch the business has expanded to over twenty shops throughout Ohio, Pennsylvania, and Indiana. While Leonard makes sure that each is worthy of the HANDEL'S name, the best place to taste Alice's original recipes is still the little shack on the busiest alley in town. Each shop makes its ice cream on a daily basis, insuring that favorites, including the **butter fudge** and world's best **chocolate pecan**, are always creamy marvels. In addition to its regular flavors, the shop is known for its unique seasonal specialties such as the **girl scout thin mint** and **banana cream pie**. The shop even has HANDEL'S-brand coins and certificates — needless to say, this change is as good as currency in this town.

GLOSSARY

It seems like every ice cream parlor has a unique terminology to describe the flavors, concoctions, and general goings on at their shops. This glossary highlights the terms that have caught on either regionally or nationally and have become a part of the ice cream lexicon.

Banana Split — The most popular of all sundaes, it consists of a banana, sliced lengthwise, layered with three scoops of ice cream, a sauce or multiple sauces, whipped cream, and a maraschino cherry.

Boston — A shake or malt topped with a sundae.

Brain Freeze / Ice Cream Headache — An intense headache caused by the application of a cold substance, i.e. ice cream, to the roof of one's mouth.

Cabinet — A Rhode Island term for a milkshake.

Check the Vanilla — A communication among ice cream servers to take a look at an attractive customer who just came into the shop.

Concrete — A mixture of frozen custard blended with candy or fruit. A true concrete is much thicker than a shake and can be turned upside down for at least a minute without dripping.

Cooler — A shake with soda water.

Float — A soda containing scoops of ice cream. A milkshake float contains an extra scoop of ice cream added after the mixing process.

Frappe — A Boston and eastern Massachusetts term for a milkshake.

French Ice Cream — Ice cream made with a cooked custard base.

Frozen Custard — Ice cream that is not hard frozen and contains at least 1.4 percent egg yolk solids (for more information see page 46).

Frozen Yogurt — A low-fat treat that contains cultured dairy ingredients as well as sweetening and flavoring ingredients.

Gelato — Italian ice cream, gelato is usually made with milk, water, or soy as a base, and contains only the amount of air that is naturally incorporated during the churning process. The resulting low butterfat content (between 0 percent and 10 percent) and minimal overrun (less than 30 percent) makes for a healthy, dense, and intensely flavorful treat.

Granita — Nearly frozen crushed ice drinks flavored with various syrups; some versions and almost all coffee renditions are layered between dollops of whipped cream.

Italian Ice / Water Ice — A frozen mixture of water, sugar and liquid flavoring. Lemon is by far the most common flavor.

Jimmies / Sprinkles — Tiny rod-shaped, crunchy candies commonly used as a topping for ice cream. The ice cream public is split on whether jimmies should only refer to chocolate versions or, like sprinkles, can be used for any color. Also known as decorettes, essemets, and shots.

Kulfi / Khulfi — Indian ice cream, made with boiled milk and ingredients such as cardamom, mango, pistachio, and saffron.

Ladybug — An attractive, dapper male ice cream server around whom female customers like to gather.

Malt / Malted — A mixture of milk, ice cream, malted-milk powder, and a flavoring such as chocolate or vanilla.

Milkshake — A blended combination of ice cream and milk, often containing a flavored syrup, fruit, or other flavorings.

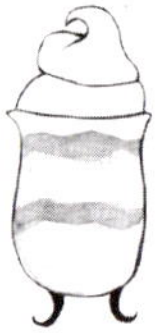

Parfait — Ice cream layered with flavored syrup or fruit and whipped cream.

Sherbet — A mixture of fruit juices (or sweeteners), water, and milk. Sherbet is lighter than ice cream, with a butterfat content between 1 percent and 2 percent, but still maintains a creamy texture.

Side car — The scoop of ice cream floating in a root beer or cola float.

Smoosh-in / Mix-in — Ice cream smooshed, mixed, or mashed on a hard service with a customer's choice of nuts, candies, fruits, or other ingredients.

Soft Serve — Ice cream that is served straight from the machine, before any freezing or hardening processes. Typically soft-serve ice cream is made with milk, not cream, and is thus lower in fat.

Sorbet / Sorbetto — Similar to sherbet, but made solely from juices or sweeteners, resulting in a flavorful nondairy treat.

Sundae — One to three scoops of ice cream, topped with one or more sweet sauces and various other ingredients including fruit, nuts, and whipped cream. Popular versions include the banana split (see definition), the tin roof, the turtle, and the dusty road. See page 77 for additional information.

New terms spring up every year and some may have been left off, so please send us an e-mail at **lingo@happybellyguides.com** if you would like to submit an ice cream expression for future glossaries.

SPECIAL THANKS TO STEVE HERRELL AT HERRELL'S IN NORTHAMPTON, MA, FOR ALLOWING US TO USE SOME DEFINITIONS AND EXPRESSIONS FROM HIS ICE CREAM DICTIONARY (ACCESSIBLE AT WWW.HERRELLS.COM).

INDEX BY SECTION

INDEX BY SHOP

PHOTOGRAPHY CREDITS

Photographs that are the property of individuals or businesses other than author follow:

Cover, pp. 8, 96: Beverly Poppe
pp. 59, 79, 90, 99: Richard Cress
Full-page opposite p. 1, pp. 32, 33: Rachel McGarry
p. 48: Johnny Trimble
p. 51: Shannon Jackson Arnold
p. 11: Courtesy of Central Dairy and Jim Dyke
pp. 17, 47: Courtesy of Chris Richey
pp. vi, 22: Courtesy of Whitey's
p. 37: Courtesy of Izzy's and Kay Fulton
p. 56: Courtesy of Capanarri Ice Cream
p. 61 (both): Courtesy of Oberweis Dairy, Inc.
p. 68: Courtesy of Laura Hodges for the Madison Area Chamber of Commerce
pp. 70, 95: Courtesy of Young's Jersey Dairy
pp. 73, 93, back cover: Courtesy of Mallard Ice Cream and Peter James (www.pjpa.com)
pp. 83, 84: Courtesy of Graeter's Inc.
pp. 88, 91: Courtesy of Lisa Fjeld and Jeni's Fresh Ice Creams